Relationships in Chronic Illness and Disability

Renee F. Lyons
Michael J. L. Sullivan
Paul G. Ritvo
with James C. Coyne

Sage
Series
on Close
Relationships

SAGE Publications
International Educational and Professional Publisher
Thousand Oaks   London   New Delhi

For information address:

SAGE Publications, Inc.
2455 Teller Road
Thousand Oaks, California 91320
E-mail: order@sagepub.com

SAGE Publications Ltd.
6 Bonhill Street
London EC2A 4PU
United Kingdom

SAGE Publications India Pvt. Ltd.
M-32 Market
Greater Kailash I
New Delhi 110 048 India

Printed in the United States of America

Library of Congress Cataloging-in-Publication Data

Lyons, Renee F.
   Relationships in chronic illness and disability / by Renee F.
Lyons, Michael J. L. Sullivan, Paul G. Ritvo; with James C. Coyne.
      p.   cm.—(Sage series on close relationships)
   Includes bibliographical references and index.
   ISBN 0-8039-4703-8 (cloth).—ISBN 0-8039-4704-6 (pbk.)
   1. Chronic diseases—Psychological aspects. 2. Chronic diseases—
Social aspects. 3. Chronically ill—Family relationships.
I. Sullivan, Michael J. L. II. Ritvo, Paul G. III. Title.
IV. Series.
RC108.L95   1995
616'.001'9—dc20   95-4428

This book is printed on acid-free paper.

95 96 97 98 99 10 9 8 7 6 5 4 3 2 1

Sage Production Editor: Tricia K. Bennett
Sage Typesetter: Andrea D. Swanson

Dedication

This book is dedicated to two exceptional people, Paul Gouett and John Berg.

Paul Gouett is a resident of Halifax who, despite multiple sclerosis, has made major contributions to services for people with a disability in Canada. He has taught his friends much about personal strength, living well with a disability, and close relationships.

John Berg was Associate Professor of Psychology at the University of Mississippi. He died on May 20, 1991, at the age of 39. Despite having multiple sclerosis, he was a serious and dedicated scholar. He was a key contributor to research on personal relationships, particularly self-disclosure, loneliness, networks, social support, and social exchange in the development and maintenance of personal relationships.

Contents

Series Editors' Introduction

When we first began our work on love attitudes more than a decade ago, we did not know what to call our research area. In some ways, it represented an extension of earlier work in interpersonal attraction. Most of our scholarly models were psychologists (although sociologists had long been deeply involved in the areas of courtship and marriage), yet we sometimes felt as if our work had no professional "home." That has all changed. Our research not only has a home but also an extended family, and the family is composed of relationship researchers. During the past decade, the discipline of close relationships (also called personal relationships and intimate relationships) has emerged, developed, and flourished.

Two aspects of close relationships research should be noted. The first is its rapid growth, resulting in numerous books, journals, handbooks, book series, and professional organizations. As fast as the field grows, the demand for even more research and knowledge seems to be ever increasing. Questions about close, personal relationships still far exceed answers. The second noteworthy aspect of the new discipline of close relationships is its interdisciplinary nature. The field owes its vitality to scholars from communication, family studies and human development, psychology (clinical, counseling, developmental, social), and sociology, as well as other disciplines such as nursing and social work. It is this interdisciplinary wellspring that gives close relationships research its diversity and richness, qualities that we hope to achieve in the current series.

The **Sage Series on Close Relationships** is designed to acquaint diverse readers with the most up-to-date information about various topics in close relationships theory and research. Each volume in the series covers a particular topic or theme in one area of close relationships. Each book reviews the particular topic area, describes contemporary research in the area (including the authors' own work, where appropriate), and offers some suggestions for interesting research questions and/or real-world applications related to the topic. The volumes are designed to be appropriate for students and professionals in communication, family studies, psychology, sociology, and social work, among others. A basic assumption of the series is that the broad panorama of close relationships can be best portrayed by authors from multiple disciplines, so that the series cannot be "captured" by any single disciplinary bias.

The current volume, *Relationships in Chronic Illness and Disability,* answers a real need in both the relationships and the behavioral medicine areas. Authors Lyons, Sullivan, and Ritvo, with a valuable contribution from James Coyne, blend the literature on close relationships with that on disability and chronic illness, to increase readers' awareness of the intermeshing of health/illness and close relationships of many kinds. As they discuss the multiple impacts of illness/disability, ways in which relationships and illness/disability are reciprocally influential, methods of coping with illness/disability, interventions with relationships affected by illness/disability, and finally, the future needs of this area of study, these authors raise the reader's consciousness about the daily realities of millions of ill and disabled people and their partners, families, and friendship networks. Scholarly yet also very practical, this book is a wonderful addition to the Sage Series.

CLYDE HENDRICK
SUSAN S. HENDRICK
SERIES EDITORS

Preface

Each of the authors of this book had a slightly different motive for wanting to write it. However, we all had confronted the relationship challenges of chronic illness and disability in our clinical and community work and held a common view that a book on relationships and disability had to be written. My experience in counseling and community development for people with chronic illness and disability in rural and urban Nova Scotia had repeatedly brought me face-to-face with people of varying disabilities struggling with their places in the social lives of their families and communities.

On one hand, social isolation, perceived rejection and stigma, and loneliness were all too prevalent. Hostility and frustration were also present in overburdened family caregivers, whose own relationships were being adversely affected by their role. On the other hand, I was also exposed to people with serious health problems and disabilities whose social lives had actually improved as a result of their health problems. Some people had maintained a circle of extremely committed and supportive friends and family and were highly skilled at adapting their relationships to their health problems.

I became very curious about the relationship dynamics of illness and disability. There were lessons to be learned about life events and relationship problems from this population. There was also knowledge to be gained about the coping skills and the social adaptability of people in the face of substantial stress.

This volume addresses the interpersonal dynamics of chronic illness and disability specific to close relationships. It focuses on adults with acquired physical illness and disability. These are people who are essentially in good health, but during late adolescence or adulthood acquire an illness or injury such as a stroke, head injury, multiple sclerosis, cancer, arthritis, or heart disease. We dissect the relationship dynamics produced by illness. As personal networks change to accommodate illness, specific relationships with friends and family also change. Also discussed are the salient illness, contextual, and relational factors that may influence the nature of relationship change, as well as the contributions that various theoretical and methodological orientations have made to understanding the illness-relationship paradigm.

In Chapter 1, the reader is introduced to illness and disability and to a framework for examining three interactive relationship-illness processes: relationship change, relational supports and stresses, and relationship-focused coping. In Chapter 2, the stresses of illness and disability are explored in terms of how they affect the person with the condition and significant others. In Chapters 3 through 5, each of the three relationship processes identified in the relationships and disability framework is discussed using findings from both qualitative and quantitative research. Chapter 6 examines interventions to facilitate marital and family relationships that are dealing with chronic illness and disability. This chapter has been aptly written by James C. Coyne, a clinical psychologist with extensive experience in the area of family relationships and disability and someone who has contributed extensively to the body of knowledge on the psychosocial side of health problems. In Chapter 7, several theoretical and methodological issues are presented that merit attention in order to enhance our understanding of close relationships. In covering these topics, we hope to contribute to an understanding of the relational processes around illness and disability and, more generally, to knowledge about relationship processes and significant life events.

This is one of the few academic books that ventures into the area of relationships and illness/disability. In trying to make broad sweeps of diverse literatures, many valuable topics have been virtually ignored or omitted. The specific relationship challenges of particular health problems are not addressed. Many specific types of relationships (e.g., work, parent-child, sibling, dating partners, family, patient-health professionals) or specific relationship processes such as divorce, friendship development, or termination, are not examined in detail. Methods of relational need assessment are not discussed. The range of possible interventions, such as friendship-matching programs, relational/social skills development, and support groups, are largely excluded, and we apologize for the omission of these important topics. A lengthy reference list is provided that may be helpful to those who wish to pursue some of these topics.

Writing a book with others is a relationship story in and of itself. The Hendricks and the **Sage Series on Close Relationships** had given us an enormous opportunity. The first book meetings with coauthors Michael Sullivan and Paul Ritvo were exciting as we began creating grand theories to explain the relationship experience of disability. As time passed, however, we struggled with the realities and practicalities of how this complex topic could be tackled. None of us had ever written a book, but we were all experts on how it should be done. Through our initial writing efforts, we discovered many things about ourselves. The three of us had totally different writing styles. There were spirited discussions about the relative value of qualitative and quantitative studies. There was disagreement over whose work was important and how we should present the various bodies of literature on coping and support, relationships, and life events. It was a challenge to organize the tasks of writing. An edited text would have been so much easier in this regard.

We realized how differently each defined close relationships. Questions that we asked ourselves about how *we* would respond to various health challenges brought us to very different perspectives based on our own relationship experience, our experience with disability, academic upbringing, and, perhaps, our gender. There were times that we did not talk much to one another and times where we all felt we were on an impossible journey. At a particularly low point, I met Jim Coyne and was inspired by his work on couples coping with cardiovascular disease. So I asked him to write the chapter on interventions. Then we were absolutely committed. The book had to be finished. In the end, each of the coauthors made important contributions to the book. We sincerely hope that our struggles and persistence will spawn useful insights, increased relationship research on the topic of illness and disability, and attention by the health care field to the relationship side of health problems.

A little stress is completing a book. A big stress is addressing the challenges of disability. Because two of us live in Nova Scotia, and another one did, and all four of us like folk music, it seemed appropriate to end by addressing the issue of disability with some lines from the late Stan Roger's song, "The Mary Ellen Carter." The song tells the story of individuals who battle seemingly insurmountable obstacles to raise a sunken ship. The final message in the song is as follows:

> And you to whom adversity has dealt the final blow,
> With smiling bastards lying to you everywhere you go;
> Turn to and put all of your strength of arm and heart and brain
> And like the Mary Ellen Carter, rise again!
> Rise again! Rise again!
> Though your heart it be broken and life about to end,
> No matter what you've lost—be it a home, a love, a friend—
> Like the Mary Ellen Carter rise again.[1]

RENEE F. LYONS

✎ Note

1. Verse reprinted by permission. All rights reserved. Fogarty's Cove Music, copyright © 1979.

Acknowledgments

Many people were instrumental in making this book happen. We wish to thank Susan and Clyde Hendricks, Terry Hendrix, and Sage Publications for giving us this opportunity, for their useful suggestions, and for their patience. We also thank Steve Duck, Miriam Stewart, and Kristin Mickelson for their reviews of earlier drafts. A special thanks goes to Darlene Meade, a Dalhousie graduate student whose focus group research on women with multiple sclerosis contributed to the collection of personal accounts in this book, and to all of the respondents with health problems and disabilities who helped us clarify the personal and relational experience of disability. Thanks are extended to Andrea Trueman, Geoffrey Lyons, Tara MacDonald, and Shirley Wheaton, who helped with the references and clerical tasks. And last but not least, sincere thanks to our partners and family members who supported us through this endeavor.

1

Relationship Processes in Chronic Illness and Disability

 ew relationships in adulthood remain untouched by health
problems. Serious health problems challenge the quality and
maintenance of relationships with family and friends at the same
time that such relationships play a pivotal role in coping with
illness. This book examines the impact of chronic, disabling health
problems on relationships with family members and friends. We
identify relationship and social network changes that occur as a
result of illness and disability, and discuss why some relationships
adapt remarkably well to health problems and others do not. For
those with an interest in the study of personal relationships, the
presence of illness and disability provides an important venue for
examining relational processes through the experience of stressful

life events. The book also addresses the roles that friends and family play in coping with serious health problems. The individual is rarely alone in experiencing the impact of illness. Although this fact may be most evident in the literature on caregiver burden, illness and disability can be a major stressor for partners, children, parents, and friends.

The intrusion of illness and disability into the relational life of a couple is introduced by the story of Eleanor and Gary.

❧ The Story of Eleanor and Gary

Gary and Eleanor are in their early forties. They live in a small, seaside community about a half-hour's drive from the city and their places of work. They have a 1-year-old adopted son. Gary is an entrepreneur who enjoys the challenges and risks of operating his own business. Eleanor is a bank executive who has been promoted through the ranks to her current managerial position. Although busy with work during the week, Gary and Eleanor spend time on weekends fixing up their property, playing golf, parenting, and socializing with family and friends.

Two years ago, Gary's mother, who had been responsible for much of the kinkeeping in her large, close-knit family, was diagnosed with pancreatic cancer. Every other weekend, Gary and Eleanor made the 6-hour drive to the village where Gary's parents lived to visit his ailing mother, provide support to Gary's father, and relieve his brother and sister-in-law from caregiving. The mother's health deteriorated quickly, and, just 8 months after diagnosis, she died. Not only was this a substantial loss for the family, but it left Gary's father without the stability and support he required. He had experienced several strokes prior to his wife's illness, and although he had made remarkable physical recoveries, he had depended heavily on his wife because of residual cognitive difficulties, particularly forgetfulness. He felt lost without his wife.

For the next year, Gary's father took turns living with each of his four children, including Gary and Eleanor. Although Gary and

Eleanor were initially quite willing to accommodate him, they hadn't realized the extent of his cognitive problems, including the need for order and consistency. When things didn't proceed as expected, such as the meals being on schedule or conversations being interrupted by the baby, he had little tolerance. He would lash out at Eleanor, criticizing her performance as a mother and her "overcommitment" to her work instead of her family. She resented his intrusion into her work and family life, and found it difficult to conceal an increasing hostility toward her father-in-law for the disruption he was causing.

Just as stressors had reached the boiling point, Gary's father moved on to another sibling's home. Shortly afterward, however, he died suddenly of a heart attack. His children attributed his death primarily to a "broken heart" associated with being unable to reestablish a meaningful place within the extended family. The children had felt helpless in addressing this issue.

With the health problems of his parents behind him, Gary was almost immediately faced with the added responsibilities of single parenthood. Several surgeries required Eleanor to spend time in the hospital and to obtain a leave of absence from work to recuperate. Eleanor's career was placed on hold. Many of the pleasurable activities Gary and Eleanor enjoyed individually and as a family were reduced or eliminated because of Eleanor's pain. Both were forced to conserve energy to tackle the basic maintenance requirements of work, home, and caregiving. Daily life and plans for the future became increasingly contingent on health issues.

The complex interaction between close relationships and disabling health problems is illustrated in the story of Eleanor and Gary. First, there was the impact of cooperative efforts of committed family members to provide care and support to their parents. These efforts necessitated adjusting everyday routines to accommodate extensive support functions. Second, the loss of Gary's mother created a large void in the overall functioning of the extended family such that members of the family were called on to provide additional emotional and practical support to the father. The health problems of Gary's father placed a severe strain on members of his extended family, challenging their willingness and ability to manage adequately the cognitive disabilities resulting from neurological impairment.

Gary and Eleanor's relationship was disrupted by these chronic health problems that intruded on their established relationship roles and routines. Eleanor's work role was also threatened by her health problems. The situation was further exacerbated by expectations from her father-in-law that she provide the kind of support given by women who maintain a more traditional, homemaker role in which caregiving is a dominant activity. Her need to express anger and frustration with these expectations conflicted with her desire to be a "good wife." The pain she experienced also interfered with her ability to address such relationship conflicts. Commitments to family health issues also provided little opportunity for Gary and Eleanor to address issues in their own relationship and to maintain their outside friendships, which would probably have provided diversion from illness as well as emotional support in confronting these stressors.

In situations like Gary and Eleanor's, where people with serious health problems confront the challenges of preserving their identity and social roles, and where friends, mates, and families are struggling to construct a life that can accommodate illness, many compelling questions are raised. What can research reveal about the individual and relational stressors of chronic illness? How do these stressors change personal relationships? How do relationships support and constrain coping and adaptational processes? How do people maintain and adapt relationships through the experience of disabling health problems? What clinical interventions may be effective in addressing the stresssors of illness in relationships?

We begin to examine these issues in Chapter 1 by clarifying the terms *chronic illness and disability* and *close relationships*. Then we introduce the study of relationships and health problems, and a framework for examining the linkages between them. In Chapter 2, we provide an overview of the stress-creating properties of illness and their emotional effects as a prelude to three close relationship and disability themes: Theme 1, the impact of illness on personal relationships (Chapter 3); Theme 2, the effects of relationships (supports and stressors) on individuals experiencing a disabling health problem (Chapter 4); and Theme 3, relationship-focused coping (Chapter 5). These explorations are relevant to the discussion in Chapter 6 of interventions designed to facilitate relational adaptation to illness and disability. We conclude with recommendations for future directions in research in Chapter 7.

ᴥ Chronic Illness and Disability

In this book, we discuss chronic illnesses and disabilities as conditions that result in moderate to severe restrictions in physical functioning and the performance of social roles related to work, leisure, family, and friendships. The term *chronic* signifies a long-term condition encompassing a course that may be stable, unpredictable, or progressive. Examples of disabling health problems include AIDS, arthritis, asthma, cancer, diabetes, heart disease, multiple sclerosis, and stroke. There are also many chronic, disabling conditions that are not considered illnesses per se, such as head and spinal injuries, that may present substantive relationship and adaptational challenges.

Current nomenclature distinguishes three interrelated dimensions of health problems: impairment, disability, and handicap. The World Health Organization (1980) defines *impairment* as any abnormality of physiological or anatomical structure or function, for instance, difficulty in breathing. *Disability* is the limitation in ability to perform activity considered normative for a human being, such as walking or reading. *Handicap* is defined as any disadvantage for an individual that limits the fulfillment of a normal role or occupation, such as family or work responsibilities. Handicaps are substantially affected by societal values and attitudes toward disability, which influence accessibility to work, leisure, and relationships as well as the individual's attitude and adaptational capacity. These classification categories highlight important interactions between an individual's illness and physical and social demands that are placed on the individual. Impairment is defined solely in terms of disruptions in physiological or anatomical functioning. However, the defining criteria for disability and handicap point to the important roles of the physical, interpersonal, and societal environment in determining the degree of "loss" that will be experienced as a result of a specific impairment.

We limit our focus in this book to adults with acquired, chronic, physical health problems. Physical illnesses such as heart disease, multiple sclerosis, chronic pain, and cancer are by far the most prevalent forms of chronic health conditions. These health problems can result in significant life changes, including changes in established relationships. Acquired physical health problems may affect established roles, relationships, and life goals in somewhat different (although no less important) ways from mental illness or developmental disabilities (i.e., disabling health problems acquired in childhood). Table 1.1 provides a taxonomy of the more predominant acquired illnesses, impairments, disabilities, and handicaps.

The Prevalence of Disability

Dramatic changes have occurred in patterns of morbidity and mortality in North America over the past century. Average life expectancy has increased from 49 years in 1900 to more than 75 years today, and the proportion of the population 55 years and older has more than doubled (National Center for Health Statistics, 1983, 1984). Chronic health problems have largely replaced infectious diseases as the leading causes of death (Satariano & Syme, 1981). Consequently, people are living longer, but they are living longer with chronic, disabling health problems (Coyne & Fiske, 1992).

Estimates are that up to 50% of North Americans will experience chronic health problems during their lifetime (Cole, 1974). In 1991, an average of 15.5% of Canadians reported some form of disability. The proportion ranged from 7% in children under 15 years of age, to 14% in adults aged 35 to 54 years, to 46.3% in people aged 65 years and over (Statistics Canada, 1992). People over the age of 65 are likely to experience multiple disabling health problems.

Table 1.1 Examples of Chronic Illnesses, Impairments, Disabilities, and Handicaps

Type of Condition	Impairments	Disabilities	Handicaps
Cardiovascular	*Sensory*	*Restricted Abilities in*	Educational, social, and community services
Angina	Hearing		
Atherosclerosis	Smell	Child rearing	
Hypertension	Touch	Driving	
Myocardial infarction	Vision	Helping others	Exclusion
	Mobility	Household chores	Financial dependence
Stroke	Bending	Learning	
Neuromuscular	Climbing stairs	Leisure	Inadequate recreational, employment, housing, health, and rehabilitation
Arthritis	Lifting	Self-care	
Back pain	Manual dexterity	Sexual performance	
Epilepsy	Running	Speaking	
Huntington's chorea	Walking	Walking	
Multiple sclerosis	*Cognition*	Work	Lack of respect/social value
Parkinson's disease	Attention span	Writing	
	Information processing		
Post-polio syndrome	Memory		Lack of respite and other supports for caregivers and family
Auditory & Visual Problems	*Emotion/Affect*		
	Depression		
	Moods/irritability		
Cancer	*Other*		Physical and social isolation
Breast & cervical	Atypical appearance		
Hodgkin's disease			Physical inaccessibility
Skin	Breathing difficulties		Segregation
Respiratory Conditions	Communication problems		Stigma/ stereotyping
Allergies	Fatigue		
Asthma	Pain		
Emphysema	Numbness		
Traumatic Injuries	Weakness		
Amputations			
Head injury			
Spinal injury			
Immunological & Other			
AIDS			
Chronic fatigue			
Diabetes			

ᴕ Close Relationships

Humans seem to require a variety of relationships that contribute in different ways to well-being (Hirsch, 1980; Walker, MacBride, & Vachon, 1977). One means of distinguishing close relationships from other social connections is the manner in which people describe members of their social networks. In clarifying these distinctions, Milardo (1992) identifies four basic types of social networks that people maintain. Our *global* network encompasses all of the people we know. *Interactive* networks include those with whom we usually interact. *Exchange* networks include people who provide, or who are expected to provide, material support to each other. A fourth category, the network of *significant others and intimates*, typifies the notion of close relationships. This network contains people considered most important, such as spouses, lovers, family members, kin, and close friends.

What makes a relationship close? There have been many attempts to characterize the qualities valued in close relationships through research on intimacy, attachment, and social support (e.g., Cobb, 1976; Cohen, Mermelstein, Kamarck, & Hoberman, 1985; Floyd, 1994; Weiss, 1974). Weiss (1974) proposed that relationship provisions include attachment, social integration, reassurance of worth, reliable alliance, guidance, and opportunity for nurturance. When asked to describe their friendships, people indicate positive states such as trust, affection, mutual respect, acceptance, loving, and caring (Parks & Floyd, 1994). People tend to opt out of friendships if the friend is no longer liked, is not pleasing to be with, or does not provide social validation (Duck, 1991; Rawlins, 1992). Characteristics of close relationships may be based on the relational descriptor used for closeness. For instance, Monsour (1992) found that self-disclosure was a central and consistent provision of relationships when people were asked about their "intimate" relationships.

Do people have a clear set of relationships that they consider close? Evidence exists for some temporal stability in identifying network members considered to be close relationships. People seem to be fairly consistent in identifying their close relationships over time (Broese van Groenou, van Sonderen, & Ormel, 1990; Milardo, 1992; Rapkin & Stein, 1989). This stability, however, does not mean that close relationships are impervious to life change or life stress. The research suggests that although close relationships may be maintained across different life events and transitions, their *character* or *nature* varies significantly as a function of changing circumstances, such as marriage, parenthood, or relocation (Kimmel, 1979; Newcomb & Bentler, 1981; Steuve & Gerson, 1977). Most relationships in life are imposed in some respect; however, people can usually opt out of friendships more easily than kin relationships.

With respect to close relationships and illness, obligations for dealing with the day-to-day practical aspects of illness have been traditionally assigned as family responsibilities, particularly for women. The role of friends in such obligations is less clear. Friends have been assigned more companionate, socializing roles, such as support of a positive outlook. However, in today's society, societal family-friendship roles have become less distinct. Societal changes have occurred in the roles and functions of nuclear and extended families. There is reduced geographical proximity, and gender-defined roles are less precise. Family structural changes have occurred that include divorce and remarriage, single parenthood, blended families, and homosexual relationships. Correspondingly, relational roles with respect to illness have also become less clear. There appears to be a growing dependency on friends for support traditionally given by family. In short, although kinship is a relationship whose primary constituting feature is obligation, and the primary constituting feature of friendships is voluntary sociability, there is obviously a fusion of these roles in evolving contemporary society.

There are many relationship characteristics or dimensions that could be examined in the context of illness. Four dimensions discussed in this book are the structure, content, process, and quality of relationships. *Structure* is the collection of objective characteristics of specific relationships and networks. It can include the size of the network, the composition, the frequency of contact, power and status hierarchies, and so on (Adams & Blieszner,

1994). *Content* refers to what people do together in areas such as companionate activity, communication, social support, and social exchange. *Process* reflects the dynamic nature of relationships, including covert cognitive and affective responses, and overt behavioral changes (Duck & Sants, 1983; Kelley, 1983). *Quality* refers to the evaluative appraisal of relationship outcomes such as support, attachment, intimacy, pleasure, loneliness, and conflict.

❧ Close Relationships and Illness/Disability

Over the past 20 years, the social life of people with illnesses and disabilities has become an increasingly regular theme of books and film. In the popular literature, the topic of personal relationships and illness has appeared in numerous accounts of coping with illness, which include issues of love, stress, and support for a variety of health problems (e.g., friends coping with cancer in the film *Beaches*).

The Vietnam War created a young and visible population of physically and emotionally disabled veterans in the United States. In conjunction with the human rights movement, the aftermath of the Vietnam War led to widespread concern for the quality of life and the social integration of individuals with disabilities. The prevalent ideology over the past 20 years has been normalization and integration (Hutchison & McGill, 1992; Wolfensberger, 1972; Zigler & Hall, 1986), guided by the principle that people with disabling health problems have the right to community participation, adequate housing, work, and meaningful personal relationships. The increased presence of people with disabling health problems "on the street" has made salient the need to become more competent in social relationships with people with disabilities.

Many governments, including those in Canada and the United States, have taken significant steps to promote the integration of individuals with disabilities. For instance, Canada recently passed constitutional legislation against discrimination on the basis of physical and mental disability (Francis, Lascelles, Cappon, & Brunelli, 1993; Government of Canada, 1991). In 1991, the Government of

Canada also announced a National Strategy for the Integration of Persons with Disabilities and dedicated $158 million (Canadian) for integration programs and research.

Ultimately, however, the integration of people with disabilities is a social relationships issue. Human rights legislation may formally mandate against discriminatory practices in the community, but the extent of an individual's social integration will be based primarily on acceptance; social validation; and inclusion by family, friends, and colleagues. Legislation can influence the degree to which the workplace is physically accessible, but legislation has only minimal impact on societal values toward or beliefs about people with disabilities. The social stigma of disability continues to be a major barrier to the social integration of individuals with disabilities. Although advances in technology and increased accessibility may reduce the degree of disability associated with physical impairment, negative societal attitudes have interfered with efforts to reduce the level of handicap associated with disability. Denise Beaudry, blind through glaucoma, states:

> The two biggest obstacles as a result of blindness are a lack of job opportunities and a frequent difficulty establishing personal relationships with sighted people. Both obstacles came, I think, from the difficulty that other people have in dealing with my blindness. . . . On the personal level, people exclude me from normal social activities because they don't think I can function. They also have funny notions about what kind of lives blind people lead. I have a male friend that I live with, and people find it difficult that I can have a male-female relationship just like everyone else. Many people assume that he is my brother. They hesitate to suggest activities to me for fear that I can't participate. They just don't know the many ways that I have of doing normal activities. (Government of Canada, 1981, p. 15)

Social scientists initially used illness and disability as a testing ground for theories about social stigma (e.g., Goffman, 1963; Ladieu-Leviton, Adler, & Dembo, 1948). Early theorizing attributed difficulties in personal relationships to social discomfort created by the disability. Researchers then became increasingly interested in how coping, social support, and caregiving played a role in adjustment to illness (Barr, 1993; Coyne & Fiske, 1992; Gottlieb & Wagner, 1991). Recently, illness and disability have also become significant topics in the quest to better understand the effects of significant life changes on social network structure and function (Lyons, Ritvo, & Sullivan, 1992; Morgan & March, 1992).

Much of the research on relationships and illness revolves around two interrelated themes: (a) how disabling health problems affect close relationships and (b) how close relationships influence coping with and adaptation to health problems. In the first theme, the presence of illness and its intrusiveness on established social roles and relationship patterns marks it as a powerful influence on close relationships with family and friends. In the second theme, relationships with family and friends are implicated as a central factor in understanding coping and adaptation. One must have knowledge of who is affected, how they are affected, and the social context within which the stress is experienced and addressed (Eckenrode, 1991; Gottlieb & Wagner, 1991).

Theme (1): The Impact of Disabling Health Problems
on Relationships

There is considerable evidence that disabling health problems change relationships with family and friends (French, 1984; Janssen, Philipsen, & Halfens, 1990; Lyons, 1991; Morgan, Patrick, & Charlton, 1984; Russell, 1985; Strauss et al., 1984). In fact, relational difficulties are a major source of stress in individuals' attempts to cope with chronic illness and disability (Caplan, 1974; Cohen & Wills, 1985; Dunkel-Schetter & Wortman, 1982; Moos & Tsu, 1977). The onset of disability is frequently associated with a decrease in network size, a reduction in social contacts, and increases in social isolation and loneliness (Blaxter, 1976; French, 1984; Janssen et al., 1990; Lyons, 1986, 1991; Morgan et al., 1984). After an extensive study of the daily living concerns of adults with physical disabilities in England, Blaxter (1976) concluded that "Although the practical problems of work, money, and daily living seemed to be most prominent amongst the patients of this survey, it was social problems—family relationships, isolation, and loneliness . . . that were perhaps the most distressing" (p. 219).

Health challenges can threaten the stability of close relationships. Reductions in shared activities, the redistribution of roles and responsibilities, and changes in autonomy can strain relational bonds. Cognitive and emotional changes subsequent to a disabling health problem also affect relationships. Emotional distress, changes in role expectancies, and perceived inequities may compromise the ability to maintain satisfying close relationships. Factors such as roles, exchange and equity, distribution of power in relationships, intimacy, and relational competence have been discussed as important determinants of the development, maintenance, and termination of close relationships (Duck, 1988; Jones, Hobbs, & Hockenbury, 1982; Spitzberg & Brunner, 1991; Thibaut & Kelley, 1959).

Although we have presented disabling health problems as a major threat to relationships, there is also evidence that through even the most severe, life-threatening illness, social relationships can be preserved, effectively restructured, and even improved (Croog & Levine, 1977, 1982; Lyons, 1986; Michela, 1981; Morgan et al., 1984; Wright, 1983). Relationships are sometimes reported as closer or more valued with the threat of their loss (Henrich & Kriegel, 1961; Lyons, 1991). Provision of support and care, although sometimes defined as burdensome and as limiting personal freedom, also provides individual and societal benefits (Bar-Tal, 1984). Knowledge about the human ability to make substantial adjustments (including relationship adjustments) in response to significant life events such as serious illness may be one of the most valuable contributions of research in this area.

Illness has a way of removing the window dressing of everyday life to expose those elements that are of central importance. People often take stock of priorities, including the value they place on close relationships. Energy is reserved for people and things that really matter (Lyons, 1991). From personal accounts of the experience of disabling health problems, people have reported that the manner in which they frame their lives and their relationships is substantially changed (Wright, 1983). In a published account of B. F. Cumming's turn-of-the-century journal entries about being ill with multiple sclerosis, Murray (1992) comments:

The sombre presence of illness and impending death helped him to put life in its proper context. He was frustrated by the artificial nature of much of life. He wanted to strip away the walls, the partitions and "walk about with my clothes off, to make a large ventral incision and expose my heart." He wanted to be brutally candid with others and wanted to know everything clearly himself. (p. 59)

Theme (2): The Influence of Relationships on Coping and Adaptation

Coping and *adaptation* are terms frequently used to identify the mobilization of psychosocial and instrumental resources in response to stress (Eckenrode, 1991). Illness and disability typically introduce a number of new stresses into the lives of those with the condition, significant others, and their relationships. The influence of personal relationships on adaptation to chronic illness has been conceptualized and studied from three main orientations: the social support perspective, the stress/strain perspective, and the social support/stress perspective. The social support perspective treats personal relationships as vehicles of emotional and instrumental aid that contribute to coping with stress and to enhanced well-being (Braverman, 1983; Broadhead et al., 1983; Caplan, 1974; Cobb, 1976; Cohen & Wills, 1985; Croog & Levine, 1977; Dean & Linn, 1977; Gottlieb, 1981; Hammer, 1983; Patrick, Morgan, & Charlton, 1986). Conversely, the absence of a supportive network has been linked to loneliness and negative health outcomes (Berkman, 1985; Lynch, 1977; Reed, McGee, Yano, & Feinleib, 1983).

The stress or social strain orientation has been characterized by investigation of how social relationships impede well-being (Coyne & DeLongis, 1986; Rook, 1990). Interpersonal conflict is perceived as a major source of stress (Bolger, DeLongis, Kessler, & Schilling, 1989), with negative interactions exerting stronger and longer lasting effects than positive exchanges (Rook, 1992). Discordant marriages, for instance, can cause illness, exacerbate symptoms, or undermine adjustment to illness (Burman & Margolin, 1992). Stress may be created by unhelpful support attempts, unreliable or noncontingent support, relationship conflicts and hostility, and loss of relationships.

The combined orientation to studying relationship influences on adaptation is the stress and social support perspective fostered by the work of Coyne and DeLongis (1986), Thoits (1982), and Worchel (1984). Within this conceptualization, relationships are viewed as contributing both positive and negative outcomes in coping with illness. Coyne and Fiske (1992) assert that models of coping and social support should account for the presence of substantial illness-associated stress levels in family members as a result of illness. Actions that are considered supportive for the receiver may be stressful for the provider. This is termed *caregiver burden.* Undeniably, it is often the case that the undertaking of "giving" creates physical and mental strain on the provider. Women, in particular, appear to carry the greater burden of illness. Throughout their own illnesses, their concerns are often focused on others' well-being.

Gottlieb and Wagner (1991) point out the need for a clearer understanding of stressful situations and the relationship processes for dealing with them:

> By treating social support as a dynamic process that unfolds in particular relationships and situations, we can identify some of the contingencies governing its expression and . . . learn more about the conditions under which its protective effect is conferred. Equally important, such a process-oriented approach can offer instruction about the circumstances in which social support miscarries. (p. 165)

Gottlieb and Wagner (1991) argue that social support with respect to illness and disability should be viewed as a "social process shaped by the commerce occurring between people in particular relationships who are attempting to maintain their equilibrium in the face of conditions that are personally and socially destabilizing" (p. 166). From this "systems" perspective, coping and support are viewed in the context of relationships. Thus, in clarifying the theme of relationship effects on coping and adaptation, we suggest that relationships provide both support and stress in the coping process and that coping and adaptation processes, although traditionally studied unidirectionally in illness, are viewed as multidirectional and communal.

The two main themes described above consider the relationship as a factor in adaptation to illness, but the focus is still primarily on the individual. We believe that a complete understanding of the illness experience requires moving beyond individualistic perspectives to consider how relationships adapt to illness conditions. Understanding the illness experience means clarifying what happens to people and their relationships as a result of illness. It also directs us to analyze *what people do with what happens to them.* Indeed, this message is echoed by McCubbin and Patterson (1981) and Young (1983), who view families as *active* participants in dealing with illness, not as passive "victims" of illness.

We propose that a complete understanding of the illness experience requires consideration of *relationship-focused coping* (Coyne & Fiske, 1992). Instead of a purely individualistic orientation to coping, in which coping strategies are initiated by individuals to manage their well-being, relationship-focused coping is reflective of strategies that are initiated to address stressful life circumstances that affect relationships. These are coping strategies used to assist others in dealing with illness stressors and/or to maintain valued relationships.

There are several advantages to considering relationship-focused coping in adaptation to illness. For example, concern has been raised about the predictive capability of coping to explain outcome variability (Pearlin, 1991). One method of increasing the predictive power of coping may be to acknowledge a broader range of coping strategies or potential coping strategies employed by individuals, dyads, and groups. How individuals and their significant others cope will influence relationships. How dyads, families, or other social groupings, such as support groups, deal with problems communally will affect relationships.

◆ Framing Relationship Processes in the Context of Illness/Disability

An interactional framework for examining close relationship processes in the context of chronic illness and disability is pre-

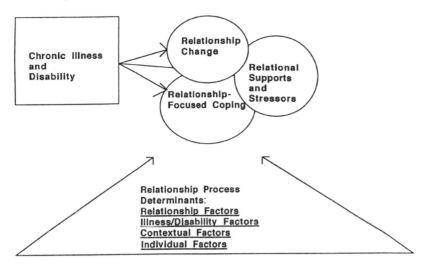

Figure 1.1. Relationship Processes: Illness and Disability

sented in Figure 1.1. This framework is adapted from Newcomb's (1981) model of the cohabitation process in which research on determinants of relational maintenance are organized around individual, dyadic, and contextual factors.

The three processes are identified within this framework: (a) relationship change, (b) relational supports and stressors, and (c) relationship-focused coping. They are all reciprocally interactive and influenced by similar interactive components that include: (a) the *Illness/Disability*—characteristics of the condition, functional and lifestyle changes, and emotional impact; (b) the *Relationship*—current and preexisting characteristics of the relationship and the network; (c) the *Individual*—sociodemographics and psychological characteristics of the individual with the health problem and significant others; and (d) the *Context*—situational and societal factors, such as social stigma, social policies, and support services, and social norms surrounding the rules and roles of relationships. These components are discussed throughout the book as we examine each of the three relationship processes as well as interventions.

In this chapter, we have provided an overview of the prevalence and intrusiveness of chronic illness for individuals and their relationships with family and friends. We have introduced the study of close relationships through illness and disability and provided a framework for examining the linkages between relationships and health problems. In Chapter 2, we proceed to clarify stressors associated with illness and disability for individuals with such conditions and their significant others.

2

The Stressors of Illness and Disability

Julie was 22 years old when she was diagnosed with multiple sclerosis (MS). She had been working as a singer in a country band and had noticed increased difficulties in maintaining the energy needed in her performances. When she first consulted her physician, Julie was told that the symptoms were the result of stress and that some rest and time off were needed.

One morning, Julie awoke and panicked when she realized that she was unable to move one of her legs. She described the sensation as a deep numbness, as if her leg were dead. Julie was taken to the hospital. Within hours, normal sensation returned to her leg, and she was walking independently.

Medical test results were suggestive of MS. To Julie, that did not mean very much. She knew a woman in her neighborhood who had MS, and she looked quite well. However, Julie's illness was to become much more severe than her neighbor's. Over the next 3 months, Julie had three major attacks of MS. The first left her with a staggering gait. With the second, she lost considerable control over her vocal cords, and after the third, she required the use of a wheel-chair. Julie always noted that of all the things MS did to her life, the loss of her ability to sing was the most difficult adjustment.

At 25, in a wheelchair, with a significant speech dysfunction, Julie did not hold great optimism for her future relational life. She had hoped for marriage and a family, but no longer saw these as realistic options in her life.

Julie had a very pleasant and outgoing style, which facilitated meeting new people. She noted, however, that people were gen-erally afraid of disabilities. In bars or during other social gather-ings, she often felt like an outsider, looking at people who were living lives very different from hers. Julie once remarked that when you have difficulty speaking, people tend to think that you are retarded. It's difficult to impress a man when you seem to be gagging on every word you try to say.

Julie had a number of casual relationships in the second and third years of her illness. She reflected that even the nicest men were afraid of becoming serious—after all, who wants to spend the rest of one's life taking care of a disabled woman? Julie once reflected that men have difficulty making love to someone with a disability. "You should see their faces when my legs start shaking. I'm thinking about sex and they're thinking about taking me to the hospital."

In her fourth year of illness, Julie moved back to her parents' home because she was unable to live independently. As her symp-toms increased in number and severity, even basic hygiene seemed like an insurmountable task.

Julie's parents were supportive and never expressed any con-cerns about her return, but Julie had considerable difficulty deal-ing with her loss of independence. She once noted that it was like being 5 years old again. "You can't wash. You can't dress yourself.

You can't even go to the bathroom without help. It does great things for your self-esteem."

In final discussions, Julie began to express her wish for institutional placement. She explained that her parents were getting older and that she felt they would not be able to really enjoy their retirement if they had to care for her. "It's not that I'm feeling sorry for myself, but really, it's my illness and I don't think my parents should have to pay for that."

In the story of Julie, living with a chronic health problem is identified as a continuous process. The process varies with the course of illness and the psychosocial response to the illness. Despite a broad range of adaptational challenges to health problems relating to diagnosis, nature, illness course, severity of symptoms, treatment procedures, concealment, and prognosis (French, 1984), there are several common properties that contribute to stress. In this chapter, illness and disability stressors are presented along with accounts of how they affect everyday functioning, personal identity, and well-being. We have organized these stressors into two interrelated domains, the *disability* and the *handicap*. These domains distinguish the issues created by the impairment itself from those created by societal factors, such as attitudes toward disability and social change. Quotations have been abstracted from qualitative studies of disability, not for the purpose of generalization, but to provide phenomenological insights into the human experience of disabling health problems.

⠶ The Disability

The Diagnosis

One of the initial stressors of a disability is the diagnosis. The term used to describe the disability will typically carry some indication of severity, time course, and prognosis. The precise meaning of the term will differ across individuals. In the story of Julie, her reaction to the diagnosis was one of relative indifference. Her neighbor had MS and appeared only minimally impaired. For others, the term provided for their disability may carry images of pain, loss, and death.

> I remember the neurologist was sitting behind his desk, looking down at my chart. I knew that the test results showed something, but I wasn't sure exactly what. I didn't really believe that it was serious. The neurologist said it was ALS. He didn't even look up. He then pronounced what the letters stood for. I still can't say it right. He still didn't look up. It was as if he was apologizing to me. "My God, I thought. What could be so terrible that he couldn't even look at me." I don't remember another word he said to me. It's all a blank. I walked out of his office thinking: "ALS, I have ALS. I remembered a movie I saw about a baseball player who had ALS. I could see him choking on his saliva, in a chair, gasping for air. That's what I could look forward to." (M. J. L. Sullivan, personal communication, March 16, 1993)

As is the case with many disabilities, a period of uncertainty may precede diagnosis. Until recently, patients experiencing the onset of MS may have waited several years before a diagnosis could be confirmed. When dealing with the stress of diagnostic uncertainty, particularly the implication that symptoms may be psychiatric in origin, a diagnosis of MS can be associated with some degree of relief.

> I was twenty years old and two months when I started getting it and they couldn't diagnose me until three years later. I was just a neurotic woman doing all those things to get attention. Take three Valium a day and you'll feel fine. (Lyons & Meade, 1993b, p. 34)

Chronicity

Chronic illness is not simply a singular event, but rather, it signifies a set of complex processes that develop and endure over time, perhaps for the rest of one's life. Zola (1981) explains how difficult it is to communicate the experience of chronicity:

> Our lives or even our adaptations do not center around one single activity or physical achievement but around many individual and complex ones. Our daily living is not filled with dramatic accomplishments but with mundane ones. And most of all, our physical

difficulties are not temporary ones to be overcome once-and-for-all but ones we must face again and again for the rest of our lives. That's what chronic means! (p. 143)

Symptom Course

Disabling health problems are frequently associated with uncertainty and unpredictability in symptom course and prognosis. In conditions such as arthritis and MS, the number and severity of symptoms can fluctuate on a daily basis. Some investigators have suggested that an unpredictable course of disabling symptoms and lack of control of the symptom course may be two of the more stressful aspects of disability (Devins & Seland, 1987).

> It's funny. A really good friend of mine has MS and she's in her mid-forties. She's got a perfect name for MS—Mighty Strange Disease. It sure is. You don't know what's coming next. You know, one day you're fine, the next day you're in a wheelchair then when you're over the attack you're back like there's nothing wrong and then you're back to a cane and it's cycle, cycle, cycle. Mighty strange. (Lyons & Meade, 1993b, p. 34)

Physical Discomfort

Pain and discomfort frequently contribute to the disability experience. Types of physical discomfort include chronic pain, reactions to treatment procedures such as chemotherapy or surgery, side effects of drugs such as antispasmodics or analgesics, fatigue, skin ulcers, and tremors. A statement from a study of nurses with disabilities (Pohl & Winland-Brown, 1992) provides an account of the impact of chronic pain on self-image:

> When you live in chronic pain . . . it changes your personality a lot! From being a very active productive member of my family, very proud of my job, I became this housewife (who) got fat, depressed and crabby. If this isn't going to end, who wants to live like this? Your whole image changes of what you are. My image was to be a very confident, functioning human being who was helping other people, which is very important to me—to nurture, to help. I need to be productive again! (p. 34)

The Disruption of Everyday Routines by Health Care

The symptoms of many disabling health problems require on-going medical care. Even when a disability is not associated with an active illness process, such as in spinal injury, disabilities are nevertheless associated with higher risk of developing medical complications (e.g., ulcers). Medical treatment can consume a person's life. Getting to and from the hospital, procedures such as kidney dialysis, and home treatments can leave little time or energy for the roles of everyday life. Life is often put on hold waiting for surgery, treatment, and recovery. The following account provides a perspective on the disruptiveness of treatment procedures from a mother with an infant with cystic fibrosis:

> I left the hospital with my daughter very confident in my abilities. . . . By the third week of being home I was fatigued and lonely. Yes, aerosol and physio 3-4 times a day was part of my routine, but that was also my *whole* day. Outings were short otherwise they disturbed my routine. . . . I also noticed my friendships changing. The lonely routine was too much to adjust to. Since no one had warned me of this daily monotony and everyone was so "up" at clinic visits, I was convinced it must be me. (Lyons & Langille, 1995)

Functional Loss

Disability, by definition, entails a reduction or loss of function and difficulty in performing activities of daily living. Chronic illnesses may involve functional limitations in mobility, fine and gross motor coordination, sensory deficits, speech and communication difficulties, performance restrictions because of pain and fatigue, and cardiorespiratory problems (Marinelli & Dell Orto, 1984) (see also Chapter 1, Table 1.1). For example, the following focus group discussion is an account of several functional limitations in grooming as a result of having MS:

> Another thing that has changed is my appearance. The way that I dress . . . some fads that come out like shoes. Well you have to. I know myself and I notice other people. I've been checking underneath the table . . . flat shoes! High heels are no way . . .

High heels are gone!

And just like our clothes. We go and instead of messing around with those little, little, tiny buttons where you're all thumbs—pull on stuff. Something easy to get on and get it off. And another thing—jewelry . . . the neck pieces . . . I can't get the clasp done.

Some earrings I can't get. The one's now that you have to get through the hole? Like the loop thingy.

And another thing—hairdos. Like we can't go and sit there with a curling iron, not anymore. You'd burn your scalp half to death and your fingers.

So, it's wash and go.

Yeah, and forget about putting makeup on. Try to put on mascara and you get it in the eyeball. (Lyons & Meade, 1993b, p. 35)

A respondent from another study on the effects of multiple sclerosis tells how a reduction in mobility affects her:

And then you wake up the next day and you find out something is harder to do. Maybe your hands are not working like they used to. Maybe you go and get into the tub and you find you can't get out. (Russell, 1985, p. 32)

Loss of functional abilities associated with disabilities frequently negatively affects social roles, such as the individual's ability to maintain employment. Eight million Americans between the ages of 16 and 64 have reported that they are unable to work because of disability (U.S. Bureau of the Census, 1986). A recent study (Pal, 1992) of the employment status of 3,200 persons with physical disabilities in the Province of Ontario, Canada, found 80% of these persons unemployed, with only 14% reporting a reasonable chance of finding employment.

In a focus group study of mothers with MS (Meade, 1994), six out of eight participants reported that they had left their jobs as a result of MS, and one participant was currently considering a leave of absence because of a recent illness exacerbation:

I have the job of my dreams . . . the one job I really wanted. And there are times when I find that really hard to come to grips with. I spent a lot of time getting into the position I'm in, and it combines so well with my family life. (p. 63)

Another woman working outside of home emphasized the income required to support herself and her daughter:

> The trouble is I have to work. If I don't work, if I'm on disability [payments], I lose my house. R. (her mate) makes $20,000 a year and we'd live below the poverty line. So, I also have the financial pressure. If I'm not working we don't really eat that well. And I don't have my house. It's not much of a house to begin with, but . . .
>   Others in the group responded: "It's yours." (Lyons & Meade, 1993b, p. 35)

❧ The Handicap

Social contexts affect both the nature of ties for people with disabilities and the adaptational outcomes. To understand chronic illness and close relationships, one must clarify both the micro (social psychological) as well as the macro (sociological) stressors of living with a disabling health problem. Personal relationships researchers (and those studying emotional response to illness) often do not address the contextual nature of chronic illness (Milardo & Wellman, 1992). Variables such as social stigma are difficult to examine empirically with regard to their impact on an individual's psychosocial functioning or on relationships. However, such variables may affect both directly by limiting the range of adaptational options. If I have a disability, I can only move toward adaptation to the extent that my social environment can adapt with me. Rigid, inflexible, or inaccurate social perceptions of disability not only will be stressors for me, but they will also restrict the nature and magnitude of my adaptational outcomes. I will not be able to experience "comfort" with my disability if my social environment feels uncomfortable. I will not be able to experience a meaningful life (including meaningful relationships) if my social environment dictates that I cannot. Societal issues include the social construction of disability, acceptance of variant appearance, relationship roles and rules, and disabling health problems as a substantive socioeconomic issue.

The Social Construction of Disability

The stereotypic image of life with a disability remains one of limitations. Images include pain, hospitalization, decreased pleasure, dependence, poverty, inactivity, social isolation, the inability to achieve life goals, role and status loss, and a decrease in physical attractiveness. Correspondingly, when people think of close friends or family members becoming ill, it conjures up feelings of sadness, loss, and helplessness. The presence of serious illness and disability in ourselves and significant others exposes human vulnerability around one of the most dreaded threats to well-being. The 14-year-old son of one of the authors put it this way: "Being sick is not something you want to think about until you really, really have to."

How do societal beliefs and values about disability affect relationships? Studies of attitudes toward disability have suggested that people with normative values do not tend to freely select people with disabilities as friends and have difficulty communicating with them (Eisenberg, Griggins, & Duval, 1982; Richardson, 1976, 1983; Yuker, 1983; Yuker, Block, & Young, 1966). Social stigma toward disability produces avoidance of interaction, social awkwardness, lowered expectations, and social and physical inaccessibility of opportunities for community involvement, all potential contributors to the reduction in opportunities for relationship maintenance and the development of new relationships. Stigma results, in great measure, from anxiety about the potential inappropriateness of one's social behavior in the presence of a person with a disability, and the potential of that person's negative reaction (Fichten & Amsel, 1986; Fichten, Robillard, Tagalakis, & Amsel, 1991). Research by Shears and Jensema (1969) found a very wide margin between acceptability as a friend and as a marriage partner, providing some evidence that, at least hypothetically, disability in friendship may not have the same degree of stigma associated with it as disability in marriage. Perhaps this is because of different investment and commitment norms for friendship. One can more easily opt out of a friendship as compared to a marriage.

However, much of the research on social stigma has been conducted with hypothetical situations and in laboratory settings. It has also been conducted with stimulus strangers and not with established relationships. Kleck (1969) found that initial contacts are very different from second interactions and ongoing involvement with people in wheelchairs. In addition, research on social stigma does not distinguish well between aversive attitudes to individuals with disabilities and social discomfort because of a lack of relational competence in their presence.

Increased efforts have been made to create more positive attitudes toward disability. Disability simulations (i.e., where individuals spend a day in a wheelchair) have been used to increase awareness of the challenges created by disability. However, such simulations can misfire because they often focus on the limitations imposed by disability. This focus creates increased negative emotional reactions to disability and a sense of helplessness in dealing with the physical and social environment (Wright, 1980). Facing physical barriers to buildings such as curbs, entryways, and stairs while seated in a wheelchair may increase societal awareness of mobility restrictions of wheelchairs. It may also exacerbate the fear of anticipating a chair of one's own someday.

Normalizing relationships through inclusion and accommodation is a strategy devised by Wright (1975) that reintroduces the individual with a disability into the social network through involvement in a range of typical companionate activities followed by discussions of difficult situations, accommodations that were required, and ways of making the experience enjoyable and meaningful for all parties. There need to be longitudinal investigations of attitude change over time and more research on strategies to reduce stigma (Fichten et al., 1991).

Care must be taken to account for changing social norms, such as the trend toward inclusion of people with disabilities in community life. Stability of negative attitudes should not be presumed. Ideological shifts (Wolfensberger, 1972) toward community involvement of disabled people, advances in treatment, symptom control, technical aids and assistive devices, and more physically accessible environments should eventually result in increased social integration.

The Disabling Health Problem as a Substantive Socioeconomic Issue

The ideology of integration promotes the concept that home is better than institutional living. However, this ideological stance has been taken at the same time that the availability of supports to live well at home have actually decreased. The quality of home life traditionally has been determined by women. With the changing roles of women who have been the caregivers or "kinkeepers" (Wellman & Wellman, 1992) in Western society, combining paid and household labor has reduced availability for women to "network" with family and community (Gordon & Downing, 1978; Wellman, 1985). The extent to which these support roles have been assumed by men is questionable (Shaw, 1985). It is important to consider how changes in attitudes regarding women and social support provision influence the provision of companionship and support to people with illness and disability.

With an increasingly greater chronically ill population, coupled with the successive recessions and increasing government deficits of the past decade, interest in illness has become somewhat more pragmatic. Ethical concerns about who receives care, who gives it (formal vs. informal support system), and the quality of life of people with serious health problems and their family members are becoming more and more pressing issues. People with serious health problems are remaining at home for both ideological and financial reasons. Nevertheless, little attention (and funding) has been given to research and intervention on the social side of health problems or health promotion strategies as compared with the more seductive topics of diagnosis and cure. Although it may be natural to wish for a reasonable quality of life for individuals with disabilities, we are currently living in a social climate with conflicting individual, family, and societal priorities that raise questions around such possibilities. These conflicting priorities translate into stress for the person with a serious health problem. Am I an emotional and financial burden to my family, to society? Is there sufficient money to cover my health, rehabilitation, and daily living costs? How will others have to sacrifice because of my disability?

‮ The Impact of Chronic Illness and Disability on Well-Being

Numerous Canadian and American studies of people with disabilities, using varying methodologies and samples, have documented the presence of high levels of depression, inactivity and social isolation, suicide, and a lack of hope and personal sense of meaning in the lives of people with disabling health problems (e.g., Environics Research Group Ltd., 1989; Kinney & Coyle, 1989; Lyons, 1986, 1987).

A quality-of-life study of 1,480 noninstitutionalized, disabled Ontarians (Environics Research Group Ltd., 1989) provided a disturbing profile of social isolation and inactivity among respondents. An investigation by Lyons (1986, 1987) of the social adjustment of 150 adults with spinal injury, stroke, and multiple sclerosis found that the majority of respondents had drastically decreased their level of social activity as a result of their disabling health problems and were experiencing social isolation, loneliness, and dissatisfaction with life.

One of the most extensive studies of quality of life and disability was conducted by Kinney and Coyle (1989). Structured interviews using several mental health and quality-of-life measures were conducted in the homes of 790 physically disabled adults living in Pennsylvania. Results indicated that respondents were markedly lonely and isolated, their daily lives characterized by solitary, sedentary, passive entertainment. Those who were dissatisfied with their lifestyles also tended to score low on feelings of mastery; were socially isolated; and reduced stress by drinking, eating, smoking, or excessive use of tranquilizing drugs.

Depression in Chronic Illness and Disability

Several studies have addressed the relationship between disability and emotional distress by examining the prevalence rates of major depression in target populations (see Rodin, Craven, & Littlefield, 1991, for a review). Major depression is a diagnostic label that is used to describe individuals who experience a cluster of symptoms that may include depressed mood, loss of interest, sleep and appetite disturbance, reduction in activity level, fatigue, concentration difficulties, excessive guilt, and suicidal ideation (American Psychiatric Association, 1987).

With MS, prevalence rates of major depression have ranged from 14% to 30% (Joffe, Lippert, Gray, Sawa, & Horvath, 1987; Minden, Orav, & Reich, 1987). In chronic pain populations, prevalence estimates indicate that approximately 21% of patients may suffer from major depression (Romano & Turner, 1985; Sullivan, Reesor, Mikail, & Fisher, 1992). Slightly lower prevalence rates of depression have been found in other chronic illnesses, such as end-stage renal disease, ranging from 5% (Smith, Hong, & Robson, 1985) to 22% (Lowry & Atcherson, 1979), rheumatoid arthritis (16%) (Frank et al., 1988), coronary artery disease (18%) (Carney et al., 1987), and diabetes (10%) (Popkin, Callies, Lentz, Colon, & Sutherland, 1988).

Research has also examined rates of depression in people with chronic illness and disability using self-report measures of depressive symptoms. In general, the findings of these studies have been consistent with the findings reported using diagnostic criteria. Both have showed high rates of emotional distress associated with disability and chronic illness (for reviews of this literature, see Rodin et al., 1991; Sullivan, Reesor, et al., 1992).

In summary, data from several sources support the view that individuals with disabilities and chronic illnesses are at increased risk for the development of depressive symptoms. Although considerable variation in prevalence rates of major depression has been reported, findings suggest that prevalence rates for major depression in chronic illness may be three to five times greater than that observed in the general population. Few comparisons have been made across disability populations to determine whether certain groups are at higher risk than others for the development of depressive symptoms. It is interesting to note that health conditions associated with the threat of death, such as cancer, do not appear to show higher prevalence rates of depression than more benign disabilities, such as chronic low back pain.

There are some indications that depressive symptoms may be highest in the early stages of chronic illness and show decreasing severity as the illness course progresses. Sullivan, Mikail, and Weinshenker (1992) reported that 40% of a sample of newly diagnosed patients with MS met the *DSM-III-R* criteria for major depression. This rate is at least twice that reported in some cross-sectional samples of MS patients with longer illness duration. A number of studies have reported an inverse relationship between illness duration and severity of depressive symptoms in patients with chronic pain. Love (1987) reported that chronic pain patients with major depression had an average illness duration of 3 years, whereas nondepressed chronic pain patients had an illness duration of 9 years. Keefe, Brown, Wallston, and Caldwell (1989) reported that chronic pain patients with less than 2 years of illness duration scored higher on a self-report measure of depression than did patients with more than 2 years of illness duration. Findings such as these suggest that depression may be most likely following the onset of chronic illness, when the individual is suddenly faced with a multitude of current or potential life changes. Over time, adaptational resources may be mobilized to deal with illness-related stresses, and depressive symptoms may abate.

Stage theorists (Dunn, 1975; Kübler-Ross, 1969) suggest that emotional reactions to illness may change in a systematic fashion during the adjustment process, similar to stages experienced with knowledge of impending death. Kübler-Ross (1969) suggests that individuals who are informed of terminal illness initially react with shock, and subsequently proceed through the stages of defensive retreat, acknowledgment, and adaptation. The more rigid the conceptualization of stages, the stronger the criticism that has been leveled at stage theories. Reactions to disability seem to vary considerably, and they are not related in a simple way to the properties of the impairment (Heineman & Shontz, 1984; Shontz, 1978).

Morse and Johnson (1991) have proposed a general stage model as a method of conceptualizing the illness experience. Taking the position that coping strategies are used to minimize suffering for oneself and others, these authors state that their stage framework involves the individual as well as family and friends. Stages include *uncertainty* (identifying and making sense of symptoms); *disruption* (realizing that an illness exists, relinquishing control to the health care system and family and friends); *striving to regain self* (controlling and preserving a sense of self, and renegotiating roles, setting goals, and seeking reassurance); and *regaining wellness* (taking charge and attaining mastery). The role of coping in adjustment to illness will be discussed in greater detail in Chapter 5.

Although Morse and Johnson (1991) developed this model as a result of studying acute health conditions, they suggested that it may be useful in analyzing chronic illness, where illness exacerbations may be similar to separate "coping" episodes of acute illness. However, after attempting to integrate findings of qualitative research on coping with MS and brain injury, we suggest that the issues of uncertainty and disruption are not single stages, but often the ongoing hallmarks of chronic illness, beginning with the onset of symptoms and extending throughout the course of the condition. The process is cyclical. People simply may learn to cope more effectively over time.

&. The Impact of Disabling Health Problems on Significant Others

Traditionally, the study of stress and distress in relation to chronic illness has focused on the individual with the condition. More recently, perhaps as a result of increased evidence of significant stress levels among caregivers and spouses, the focus has broadened to include the family caregiver (Barr, 1993; Gottlieb, 1992; Morgan & March, 1992), family members (Fiske, Coyne, & Smith, 1991; Turk & Kerns, 1985), and friends (Fisher & Galler, 1988; White, 1994). From the findings of five qualitative studies of illness, Morse and Johnson (1991) concluded:

> In particular, the role of the family needs to remain at the forefront of illness research. Too often the illness experience has been concep-

tualized as individualistic instead of reciprocal. Because of emotional ties, family and friends are intimately involved in and affected by the life of the ill individual and the impact that illness has on these individuals needs to be included. (p. 339)

The stress of chronic illness also exerts a substantial impact on family members. Functional losses can directly relate to major shifts in social and economic roles within a family. Reduced functional ability often means that others must assume work and family responsibilities as well as provide care. Outcomes include changes in personal relationships, work and leisure, and roles outside of the home (Stewart, 1993). Living conditions may be considerably changed with a loss of economic contributions. Hospitalization, medical treatments, and the requirement of care at home can result in everyday life being consumed with support and caregiving. Illness results in loss of pleasurable companionate activity with the ill individual and with other network members, and possible loss of desired employment for caregivers. The following is a newspaper account of a family's involvement with ALS, amyotrophic lateral sclerosis, or Lou Gehrig's Disease.

> Mr. Kaye could not survive without the constant care of his wife and daughters, Rebecca, 13, and Michella, 9. They get up in the morning, dress, bathe and shave him, comb his hair, brush his teeth, cook his meals, feed him, pour his drinks, make and answer his phone calls, take him to the toilet and even wet his lips, which he hasn't been able to lick in two years. . . .
> Because of the deterioration of the intricate system of muscles needed for him to chew and swallow, it takes Mr. Kaye's wife 90 minutes to feed him. "Dennis says he's already on life support," Mrs. Kaye says. "He's not hooked up to an actual machine, but he's got a walking, talking machine working for him." (Gooderham, 1993, p. D5)

The requirement of providing unrelenting support has been shown to severely stress caregivers (Oddy, Humphrey, & Uttley, 1978; Rogers & Kreutzer, 1984). To demonstrate the effect of a severe disability on significant others, we provide several personal accounts of living with a person who has suffered head injury. Traumatic brain injury is a health problem with a catastrophic beginning and an unpredictable course. Survivors and their families must often cope with disabilities associated with this injury for the rest of their lives because the individual is often left with memory and sensory deficits, cognitive and motor disturbances, and personality changes (Barr, 1993):

> The way he forgets things, and the way he talks. Sometimes you are so tired, you know, just running around. You'd like to have a few minutes peace, you know. And he'll talk, talk, talk. Sometimes you just get so tired of listening. I mean what he has to say is important. It's important to him, but I've already heard it all before. He's already told me. He's already explained it all to me and a while later he'll come back and tell me all over again, you know because he doesn't remember telling me. (p. 61)

> You never think you're going to be looking after your children again. You think maybe someday they'll have to put up with me, who knows. But you never put it in the reverse. And it is different to start all over again. (p. 61)

> When he was at home all the time, there were days when I just craved to be alone. I couldn't get my housework done because he'd be constantly at me. (p. 61)

> And a lot of it, too, is people around him saying that: "Oh, you're fine, there's nothing wrong with you."
> People shouldn't say that because they (the head injured) are not fine. They don't understand. They look at him, they sit down and talk to him and say: "Oh, he's fine."
> You know what I say to them? "Well, you come and live with him for two weeks and then you'll see." (p. 62)

The disability and handicap effects of chronic health problems on family, friends, and caregivers are discussed further in Chapters 3 and 4.

A Cumulative Effects Equation

In this chapter, we have attempted to clarify the types of stressors that illness and disability create, such as chronicity, unpredictability, and treatments that disrupt daily life. Beyond the condition itself, the social construction of illness and disability may substantively contribute to distress. Illness typically shrinks the opportunities of daily life and perspectives on the future. It interferes with activity patterns in work, leisure, and relational life and reduces freedom and spontaneity. All of these things affect well-being for people with the condition and significant others.

So how can the stressors of illness be consolidated as we progress to consider their relationship impact? A primary stressor—in this case, the health problem—tends to generate other secondary stressors (Pearlin & Lieberman, 1979; Pearlin, Leiberman, Menaghan, & Mullan, 1981). These stressors can become independent sources of stress, but considered globally, constitute an accumulation of simultaneous stressors. For instance, although loss of work may be the result of a chronic back problem, this change means that the person is not merely unemployed, but at home, experiencing functional limitations in many activities of daily living *and* experiencing pain. It may be helpful to conceptualize the stress of illness as the result of the *interactive* and *cumulative* effects of such components as the disability, the handicap, and emotional response. A logical equation identifying this process might be stated as follows.

Illness/disability symptoms
+ functional changes
+ lifestyle changes in work, leisure, routines
+ economic outcomes
+ psychological response to illness by the individual
and significant others
+ societal reactions to disability
→ effects on individuals and significant others

This cumulative approach to understanding illness stressors parallels the orientation to coping with life events provided by Hobfoll's Conservation of Resource Theory (Hobfoll, 1989). Stress occurs when personal resources (objects, conditions, personal characteristics, energy) are threatened or lost. The degree of stress imposed by life events is strongly associated with the availability of personal resources. As is evident in the above equation, the stress of illness contributes to a loss of resources *at the same time* that resources are required to cope with the illness.

Although disciplines such as psychology, sociology, and anthropology have sought to understand the illness experience from their particular traditions, the area still remains rather fragmented (Conrad, 1990; Morse & Johnson, 1991). Psychologists have focused primarily on individual emotional response to illness. Sociologists and anthropologists have assessed illness in terms of social roles, social integration, and societal response to illness. The health professions such as nursing and occupational therapy have been interested in issues of physical and psychosocial functioning, the efficacy of specific interventions, and quality of life (Renwick, 1992). Actual interventions to ease the impact of chronic illness usually are not addressed in a holistic fashion, such that the health system normally treats the symptoms of major dysfunction, not the individual's or family's quality of life. This means that the emotional, social, and practical day-to-day stressors of life with a disability are often left to individuals with the condition to sort out for themselves.

3

The Impact of Chronic Illness and Disability on Relationships

I spend my days alone except for my cat which keeps me company. (female, 60, multiple sclerosis)

Your friendships are greatly affected by your disability. I don't have any friends except maybe two from the predisability days. (female, 43, spinal injury)

I still have the same number of friends, but I can't understand why they aren't coming around to visit. (male, 63, stroke)

I am very lonely. Many of my good friends have dropped me. (female, 40, multiple sclerosis)

My husband was very supportive. Then he left me for another woman. I was devastated—even attempted suicide. I moved away and lost touch with old friends. (female, 54, stroke)

(Accounts of illness effects on relationships)
(Lyons, 1991, p. 223)

How do illness and disability change social networks and relationships? Life changes such as divorce, widowhood, retirement, and unemployment usually involve some reorganization of social activity and personal relationships. Possible network changes may include withdrawing from existing relationships, adjusting their character, and/or adding new relationships (de Jong-Gierveld, 1988).

Although some might argue that social adjustment to acquired chronic illness is similar to the processes involved in other life changes, illness brings a unique set of stressors to challenge relationship bonds. Stressors such as chronicity, unpredictability, and social stigma, identified in Chapter 2, may place substantial constraints on the ability to maintain and to restructure relationships. For example, using the cumulative effects equation given in Chapter 2, the persistent fatigue of multiple sclerosis results in reduced social contact and little energy for redefining and adapting social life to a severe health problem (Lyons, 1991; Lyons & Meade, 1995). Also, the extent to which family and friends provide support or cause stress to the person with the disabling health problem is not an isolated function of relationships but adds substantive definition to those relationships. Exchange and equity theorists (e.g., Clark & Mills, 1979; Foa & Foa, 1974; Thibaut & Kelley, 1959) state that reciprocity, a balance of contributions and rewards in relationships, is vital to relationship maintenance, and that people, if given a choice, will leave inequitable relationships (Roloff, 1981). Thus, although the provision of social support may be necessary and may provide positive effects on adjustment to disability, it may work toward the destruction of relationships if reciprocity is not forthcoming.

A concern with give and take, and fairness in relationships may present itself differently in various types of relationships. For instance, Clark and Mills (1979) have argued that the rules of exchange differ by the type of relationship. Those in close, caring, "communal" relationships do not conceive of prosocial behavior toward partners as they would in casual relationships. The notion of lifespan reciprocity has also been introduced (Antonucci & Jackson, 1990; Clark & Reiss, 1988). Lifespan reciprocity suggests that in-kind or immediate reciprocity is not necessary in close relationships as long as a long-term sense of balance is present. Nevertheless, it has been postulated that a concern with fairness exists in all relationships and may be especially salient with dramatic shifts in the assets and liabilities of partners (Leventhal, 1980; Murstein, Cerreto, & MacDonald, 1977; Utne, Hatfield, Traupmann, & Greenberger, 1984). A hypothesis by Hatfield, Traupmann, Sprecher, Utne, and Hay (1984) from equity theory specifically addresses this issue with respect to close relationships:

> In all relationships there are certain crisis periods. At such time of precipitous change, relationships will often become unbalanced. If couples are contacted before, during, and after crises, it is likely that couples will find the crisis period very unsettling, and will work to reestablish equity . . . or move in the direction of dissolution of the relationships. (p. 14)

The onset of serious illness provides an opportunity to examine exchange and equity theory in marriage and friendships and to clarify how rules of exchange operate in such circumstances. Exchange and equity theories would predict that relationships are dissolved or their quality reduced, or that conflicts result from a loss in exchangeable resources or unfair resource exchange (Hatfield et al., 1984).

A growing number of quantitative and qualitative studies have investigated the effects of illness and disability on social networks and specific relationships such as marriage and friendships. In addition, the topic of relationship change has been included in research on social support and coping (DiMatteo & Hays, 1981; Gottlieb & Wagner, 1991; Porritt, 1979); social stigma and disability (Jones et al., 1984); and social adjustment to acquired health problems (Derogatis, 1986; Weissman, 1975; Weissman, Sholomskas, & John, 1981). Many themes are interrelated, and it is difficult to construct a tight, organizational framework. To identify the effects of illness on relationships, we discuss changes in the *structure* of the social network, including marriage and friendship; the *content of interactions*, including communication, companionate activity, and social support; and the *quality of relationships*, including lone-liness, relational expectations, relationship functioning, marital satisfaction, and attributions for relationship change.

❧ Structural Changes in Networks

The Social Network

Network analyses of the effects of chronic illness on structural properties of relationships have shown a tendency toward the following changes:

1. Reduced network size (Janssen et al., 1990; Lyons, 1991)
2. Reduced social contact (Berkman & Syme, 1979; Morgan et al., 1984)
3. Changes in social space, that is, more companionate activities occurring in the home and neighborhood (Brent, 1982; Lyons, 1986; Morgan et al., 1984)
4. A decrease in the multidimensionality or range of interactions (Guay, 1982; Lyons, 1986)
5. Increased frequency of contacts at the onset of the condition or through hospitalization, then reduction or avoidance of contacts (Dunkel-Schetter & Wortman, 1982)
6. A reduction in social contact initiated by the person with a disability in the early stages of psychological adjustment (Strauss et al., 1984)
7. Restructuring of social networks to include other people with similar health problems and health professionals (Binger et al., 1969; Bozeman, Orbach, & Sutherland, 1955; Dunkel-Schetter & Wortman, 1982; Lyons, 1986; Morgan et al., 1984; Wright, 1983)
8. Restructuring of relationships to include people of lower status (Marinelli & Dell Orto, 1984)

The structural change reported most consistently is a reduction in the frequency of social contact (Berkman & Syme, 1979). A study by Janssen et al. (1990) assessed illness effects on the structure and function of social networks in The Netherlands through a longi-tudinal study comparing the networks of healthy adults with those of people suffering from chronic illness (ankylosing spon-dylitis [AS], a rheumatic disease affecting the spine, and Crohn's disease, an inflammatory bowel disease). The results of structured interviews and analysis of social contact time diaries indicated that network size was smaller for the respondents with chronic illness as compared to healthy respondents. The greatest reduction in network size was observed in the respondents who were more severely disabled. The networks of people with chronic illness contained a significantly higher percentage of kin compared to those of healthy respondents, suggesting that kin relationships may be more persistent through disability.

Similarly, Morgan et al. (1984) examined the network characteristics and social ties of a sample of disabled adults between the ages of 45 and 75 with a range of chronic conditions living in a Greater London borough. Respondents reported lower social contacts outside the home. Those with the smallest networks were not married, living alone, and had the highest degree of disability.

Friendship

Friendship, a desire or preference for proximity to particular people (Hartup, 1975), involves a process of acquaintance formation and the establishment of mutually satisfying relationships similar in some respects to those of marriage and family. Duck (1981) and Wiseman (1986), however, suggest that dissimilar commitment norms compel us to consider friendship responses to life events differently from family responses. Friendships are loosely structured, informal arrangements with beginnings and ends that are often indeterminable. People can be identified as friends or "old friends" without maintaining regular social contact. The measurement of friends' responses to changed circumstances has been conducted by assessing particular friendship dyads (Rose & Serafica, 1986). Also changes in quantitative (Fischer, 1982) and qualitative properties of friendship networks have been examined, such as LaGaipa's (1977) multidimensional approach based on friendship expectancies. However, few systematic analyses have been applied to the study of friendships of people with disabling health problems.

There is some evidence that friendships may be more vulnerable to termination than are family relationships. Johnson (1983) compared the friendship and kinship relationships of a sample of 167 older adults with health problems. Respondents were interviewed shortly after discharge from the hospital and were reinterviewed 9 months later so that the character of their network could be mapped over time. Friendships tended to break down because of health problems; however, friendship changes often varied as a function of the availability of family resources. Friends sometimes assumed a place in the social network normally occupied by family members and kin in circumstances where a strong, geographically close kin network was absent.

A study by Adams (1985) of the effects of poor health and physically limiting conditions on the friendship patterns of elderly women found that ill health affected the number of close friends, but in particular, it reduced the frequency of social interaction with friends. In a study by Lyons (1986) of adults with a spinal injury, multiple sclerosis, or stroke (150 respondents), 98% of respondents reported changes in the nature of their friendships as a result of their health problem. A general decrease was reported in contact with friends, and there were difficulties in relating to old friends (friends prior to the condition). There were also many respondents who reported rejection by old friends at the onset of the condition. One respondent commented, "It was difficult to deal with friends abandoning me at the onset of MS. The friends I have now are more loyal because they accept me as I am" (female, 47, multiple sclerosis) (Lyons, 1991, p. 83).

The respondents formed three distinct groups relative to relationship changes:

1. Those who expressed few changes in their relationships, were satisfied with their lives, and were well adjusted to their conditions. This was the smallest proportion of respondents (10%), who tended to be younger and who had milder disabilities that were not degenerative.
2. Those who experienced moderate to severe changes in their friendships because of their condition, but were able to meaningfully restructure their lifestyles and relationships (40%). These were primarily the respondents with spinal injuries and others who were able to maintain relatively active community lives.

3. Those who experienced moderate to major friendship changes and were not able to successfully restructure their relationships (50%). These were primarily respondents who had cognitive (stroke) or degenerative (MS) conditions, who were older, and who were primarily uninvolved in community life or activities outside of their places of residence. (Lyons, 1986, 1991)

Two thirds of the respondents felt that disability influenced opportunities for new friendship formation. Advantages included opportunities to meet people through consumer organizations and self-help groups, increased time for and increased interest in friendships as compared with predisability relationships, and the disability as a focus for relationship renewal that resulted in the reestablishment of some dormant friendships. Involvement in a new range of health-related activities, including hospitalization and therapy, resulted in new social contacts. Disadvantages included perceived social stigma, social awkwardness, misperceptions associated with disabilities, physical distance from friends, limitations on activities that could be enjoyed with others, and low self-esteem. Those with MS had the highest proportion of disadvantages, in comparison with respondents with stroke and spinal injury. Frequently expressed was the frustration that the person with the disability usually has to initiate interaction. This responsibility of having to initiate contact at the same time as one is experiencing decreased energy for personal relationships has been noted in qualitative research on women with disabilities (Fisher & Galler, 1988).

Attributions for Friendship Change. What attributions for relationship change are held by people with disabling health problems? Attributions for social behavior, regardless of the extent to which they reflect actual motives, will strongly influence emotional and behavioral responses (Baucom, 1987; Duck, 1981; Gottlieb, 1988). Personal accounts of the effects of disability on friendships were systematically reduced to positive, negative, and neutral (no values assigned) outcomes and assessed with respect to attributions for these effects (Lyons, 1986). When things went wrong with friendships, people with disabilities tended to attribute them to the disability or to negatively valued characteristics of friends. Although social stigma was identified as an attribution for friendship loss, it was accompanied by several other reasons, particularly the level of commitment by friends to the relationship and their relational competence in the presence of disability. The disabled individual's social competence in influencing the trajectory of relationship decline was not mentioned. However, when things went right for relationships, the key factors were relational competence in the presence of health problems and a strong commitment to relationship maintenance.

Limited dialogue between friends about the motives for relationship termination left the individual with the disability to speculate on a wide range of possibilities (Jones, 1970). This sort of speculation is reflected in the following statements:

> I don't know the reason why people stay away and it hurts a little. I wonder what I did. (male, 46, spinal injury) (Lyons, 1986, p. 84)

> Some of my best friends never came to see me. I heard that they didn't want to see me in this condition. (female, 33, MS) (Lyons, 1986, p. 84)

Illness Adaptation and Friendship Change. The termination of friendships may occur as a function of the withdrawal of nondisabled companions, but also the withdrawal by the person with the condition.

> Social relationships are disrupted or falter and disintegrate under the impact of lessened energy, impairment of mobility or speech, hearing impairment, body disfigurement, time spent on regimens and symptom control, and efforts made to keep secret so much about the disease and its management. It is no wonder that chronic sufferers themselves begin to pull out of activity and communication. (Strauss et al., 1984, p. 75)

The individual with a disabling health problem may choose to leave social circles that are unresponsive, frightened, or critical and move into more sympathetic social terrain (Strauss et al., 1984). French (1984) has suggested that during the process of adjustment, which includes the establishment of a "new identity," many old relationships may be dropped. Adjustment may require freedom from old ties in order to restructure one's personal identity and lifestyle, and an accompanying need to formulate new social connections as a sign of being attractive to others.

Marinelli and Dell Orto (1984), in a study of the psychosocial impact of paraplegia, found that many respondents experienced an initial reduction in social contacts and social activities. The establishment of new relationships was often based on the social setting—whether the location was physically accessible and whether it reduced or increased the stigma of disability. It was also found that paraplegics typically regained social contacts by initially associating with individuals of lower status, perhaps a form of downward social comparison (Brickman & Bulman, 1977).

Russell (1985) conducted an exploratory, qualitative study on the social impact of multiple sclerosis. Those diagnosed at a younger age were more likely to say that friends withdrew, and little effort was made by the respondent to maintain these relationships. Mutual withdrawal also occurred. The main reasons given for disengaging from the relationship were social discomfort and lack of relational competence in dealing with MS by both the respondent *and* friends. In other words, social awkwardness could occur in both parties. Older respondents made more positive comments than did younger respondents about the reactions of friends and appeared more self-confident in dealing with friends' awkwardness. They also displayed a more positive attitude than did younger respondents to the benefits of self-help groups in addressing relationship issues. However, most respondents identified themselves as socially isolated. Russell comments:

> If we desire to improve society, it is important to understand the experience of chronic illness and factors which would assist people in that situation to lead fuller lives. The option of withdrawal might seem easy, but it takes a silent toll in human alienation. Social withdrawal is seldom only the action of one individual. . . . This applies at the level of family, friends, or work. People are not anti-social by nature; but social hardship following, and perhaps sparked by, a physical hardship, contributes to this problem. (p. 68)

Marital Relationships

Disabilities related to several chronic illnesses, such as myocardial infarction, multiple sclerosis, and chronic pain, usually have their onset in the third and fourth decades of life. From this perspective, acquired disabilities are likely to be experienced within the context of a marital relationship.

Statistics suggest that disability is a risk factor for marital dissolution. Census data in Canada indicate that for individuals between the ages of 15 and 64, in 1986, 11% of the disabled population was divorced as compared to 6% of the nondisabled population (Social Trends Directorate, 1986). A study by Brown and Giesy (1986) of the marital status of people with spinal injury indicated that compared with the general census data in 1980, people with spinal injuries were more likely to be divorced or single. Data such as these highlight the negative impact that disability can bring to the marital relationship. However, these data do not add to our understanding of the factors that contribute to relationship dissolution for disabled individuals. In addition, divorce rates are in many ways only indirect markers of relationship quality. A more dynamically and process-oriented approach is necessary to elucidate the parameters of marital relationships that are influenced by disability.

Marital relationships have been discussed in terms of the interdependence between two individuals (Lewin, 1948). What happens to one individual is likely to influence the other. As a function of relational interdependence, characteristics of the relationship may undergo transformation to accommodate the changes in the partner's health and behavioral status (Kerns & Turk, 1985).

For many individuals, the onset of disability marks a life change that will be associated with decreased functional abilities and increased dependence. As a function of the increased dependence of the disabled spouse, the nondisabled spouse must frequently assume more responsibility for previously shared activities. The impact of redistribution of responsibilities on the marital relationship will depend to a large degree on how responsibilities were allocated prior to disability onset.

Examination of issues related to interdependence within the marital relationship has been one area of focus in research on disability and marriage. Increases in functional dependence by one partner entail increased demands for instrumental support and nurturance by the other partner. Depending on the severity of the disability, the nondisabled partner may be required to provide assistance with mobility-related activities, such as seating transfers, as well as more basic activities, such as dressing, feeding, and personal hygiene. In more severe cases of disability, the spouse may need to discontinue employment to become the primary caretaker.

Severe, life-threatening illness may disrupt and terminate a marriage, or it may draw partners closer together (Braiker & Kelley, 1979). These dichotomous effects have been attributed to the nature of the illness and the strength of the marital bond prior to the illness (Croog & Levine, 1977). Michela (1981) provides a conceptual model of the antecedents and consequences of marital relationships following a myocardial infarction. Antecedents include social and financial resources, patient and spousal characteristics, and prior relationship characteristics. Consequences include patient, spouse, and relationship changes; the nature of interpersonal events (i.e., how each responds to the circumstances, and how this is represented in communication and actions); and finally, the outcomes of these interactions and their causal attributions. By means of this model, Michela is able to present both the relational rewards and costs of illness, many of these rewards and costs being influenced by contextual factors unrelated to the illness itself.

Using intensive interviews with 90 adults experiencing chronic illness, Charmaz (1991) concluded that relationships with others shift and change as the ill person's time structure and daily activities change. Young children and spouses were most affected by these changes. Older spouses sometimes acted as if their marriage remained the same as before the onset of the condition. Couples drew apart if illness worked to increase their differences. Intimacy is often affected because of factors such as lack of spontaneity, having sex with a partner who has unattractive symptoms or appearance, and impotence. For instance, Charmaz (1991) provided the following quote by a respondent describing feelings of disengagement and lack of intimacy:

> I spend time with my boyfriend, but we don't seem to get along that well—we have been completely celibate for a couple of years and it's sort of like two cranky people living together, with health problems. And I don't like sports and he likes football. . . . And so I just feel like we sleep in the same bed and I don't even have any contact with him there because my legs hurt so much. It's like he sleeps on his side and he starts snoring, and I say: "Jim, I can't sleep." "What?" "You're snoring." "Well, I got asthma." And it's going on like that. (p. 63)

❧ The Content of Interactions

Interpersonal Communication

Relationships are strongly rooted in communication. However, communicative competence in the presence of illness and disability may be challenged on many levels. People with a disability may not wish to threaten their relationships by self-presentations of depression and anxiety, although this may be their emotional state. Family members or friends may be equally anxious about what to say and how to establish the appropriate tone of the conversation for fear of saying the wrong thing and potentially embarrassing themselves or the individual with the disabling health problem.

A female respondent in a study on relationships and disability by Lyons (1986) comments: "People are becoming more aware and understanding but they still say things without thinking, dumb things that hurt. You can always tell if they know someone who is disabled by what they say or how comfortable they are with you" (p. 30). It has been suggested that one's ordinary "social equipment" is inadequate to cope with the demands of interaction with a disabled person (Hilbourne, 1973). There is substantive evidence to suggest that people often find interaction with ill and disabled people distressing and tend to avoid it (Davis, 1961; Dunkel-Schetter

& Wortman, 1982; Goffman, 1963; Mills, Belgrave, & Boyer, 1984). People tend to show signs of discomfort, such as greater personal distance and earlier exits, in their interactions with people with disabilities (Kleck, 1968; Kleck, Ono, & Hastorf, 1966). Bean, Cooper, Alpert, and Kipnis (1980), in a study of coping mechanisms of cancer patients, found that although some respondents reported increased contact from friends and family through writing, telephone calls, and visits, over half described communication difficulties in these relationships. Correspondingly, Dunkel-Schetter and Wortman (1982), in a review of research on the social relationships of cancer patients, reported that discomfort in conversing with patients often resulted in ritualized behaviors of politeness and cards (i.e., visitors seem to be reading pat responses from cue cards), and oversolicitousness. In other words, people in awkward social situations may depend on a rigid list of communication "rules" that are not personalized for the circumstance. Argyle (1975) noted that discomfort in interactions may also be expressed through several nonverbal channels, such as rigid motor activity, few smiles, and greater interpersonal distance.

Why is there such communication difficulty? Social awkwardness may emanate from anxiety about which topics are appropriate for discussion, such as whether or not to focus on the illness or the future. Communication problems may be exacerbated because of lack of participation in mutually enjoyed activities. The focus of the interaction then becomes solely communicative. If the person with a disabling health problem has been generally inactive, communication may be further strained by topical limitations. The conversation pot dries up.

Cues from patients may produce avoidance by others. For instance, Harker (1972) found that some cancer patients become depressed and uncommunicative, and other people, taking their cue from the ill individual, reduce conversation or become anxious or irritated and leave. "A visible stalemate is reached" (p. 166). There may also be the presence of emotional contagion. Depressive reactions in response to a disability may produce depression in others, including family friends and health professionals, which may lead to avoidance (Frank et al., 1986).

People with a disabling health problem may have difficulty providing cues about their health that, without communication, are simply difficult to interpret or react to.

> The worst part I find in terms of relating to other people is the worse I am, the more I've been resting, the more careful I am to put on my lipstick. So the worse I am, the better I look. So I finally explained to my boss: "When I look good, like everything I have on matches, like I got my lipstick on straight, this is a very serious sign." You have to understand this means things are bloody awful when I have it all together by a quarter to eight in the morning. (Lyons & Meade, 1993b, p. 35)

It is usually considered helpful for the victims of a traumatic experience to converse about it (Hegelson, 1994); however, they may be doing this at the expense of being judged poorly adjusted (Glick, Weiss, & Parkes, 1974). We seem to have special admiration for people who "bear their cross." In fact, research by Kleck et al. (1966) indicates that there is a preference for interacting with the well-adjusted, "successful" handicapped student over the average nonhandicapped student. Thus, there may be a conflict between social adjustment and psychological adjustment if the latter includes an extended need for communication of negative feelings. Showing one's true feelings may have negative consequences for the relationship. Simpson (1982) explains it this way:

> If I whine, I will be avoided. If I attempt what others believe I will fail at doing, I will make them tense and nervous in my presence. But if I make them comfortable because I present myself as relaxed and self-confident, they will allow me to take charge and manage for myself. (p. 156)

Particular communicative behaviors of the person with a disabling health problem have been found to elicit positive responses in others. These include showing interest in the other people's activities; discussing the disabled person's achievements, such as athletic activities (Belgrave, 1984); and expressing positive views of life despite the disability (Kleck et al., 1966).

Silver, Wortman, and Crofton (1990) discuss the importance of balanced coping portrayals in influencing the course of social interactions and the subsequent nature and quality of support received from these interactions. However, there appear to be mixed findings with respect to whether coping portrayals affect social support provision, or the reverse, whether social support provision influences coping strategies (Davis-Ali, Frazier, & Krasnoff, 1994; Dunkel-Schetter, Folkman, & Lazarus, 1987; Manne & Zautra, 1989).

Companionate Activity

Companionate activity is shared activity, such as household maintenance tasks, work, school, and leisure. Once a substantive context for a relationship is changed (e.g., common work, school, or leisure activities), the maintenance of the relationship may be threatened, or at least the nature of the relationship may be changed. For instance, what happens to long-standing friendships maintained through years of involvement in a weekly old-timer's hockey game (followed by a beer or two at the pub) when one can no longer participate? Activity restrictions because of the health problem and physical inaccessibility of homes and public places place constraints on enjoyable activities (Brent, 1982). If the person with a disabling health problem does not turn up at the leisure haunts of buddies, what are the odds that these relationships will continue?

There may be a tendency by people with disabilities to avoid social situations where the symptoms might prove embarrassing, or social gatherings where the condition would have to be explained (Lyons, 1993b; Meade, 1994):

> When you think you're going to have your speech slur or not say what you want to, you withdraw and you don't want to go places and meet new people. (p. 87)

> You hate to go anywhere they're serving liquor . . . you get up to walk and your gait's not normal and they're going to look at you. Aha.
>   Whereupon others in the focus group comment: "You drank too much." (p. 88)

And you're always scared you're going to do something like your leg is going to give out or you're going to shake and people are going to question you and it's like, oh no, I have to go through this all over again! (p. 87)

Many people with disabilities can perform particular activities but by methods that may be considerably different from the way they are normally done; for instance, holding eating utensils in a restaurant with one's toes instead of fingers. A woman with severe rheumatoid arthritis states:

When I cry, people get very upset and some of them even try to stop me from doing it. What they don't realize is that crying is one of the few ways I have to get rid of physical and emotional tension. . . . It serves the same purpose for me as does swimming or running for other people. (Government of Canada, 1981, p. 11)

In activity-specific relationships, possibly more a function of male than female same-sex friendships (Caldwell & Peplau, 1982), people sometimes will choose pleasurable social activity over activity restrictions for health purposes. For example, Strauss et al. (1984) found that a respondent with cardiac problems refused to give up his weekly evening of cards with "the boys," complete with smoking, beer drinking, and late hours, despite his understanding that this could lead to further heart attacks.

High unemployment levels of ill and disabled adults result in a greater role for leisure as a means of social interaction; nevertheless, increased discretionary time does not equal increased leisure. Patterson's (1984) study of the leisure activities of people with multiple sclerosis found that although unobligated time had increased substantially, time devoted to leisure pursuits had lessened. McCarthy (1983) reported that 40% of young, disabled adults indicated church attendance as their only social activity outside of the home. Social contact scores of the more severely disabled people in a study by Morgan et al. (1984) were significantly related to lower rates of unemployment and participation in activities outside of the home. In Lyons's (1986) study, 67% of the respondents indicated that they were not working because of their condition;

nevertheless, decreases in leisure were reported in every activity category (particularly physical and outdoor activities) except peer support clubs, television, and passive social activities.

Relational difficulties expressed by working-age males in Britain who were unemployed because of health problems include a redirection of social activities to wholly female company (Blaxter, 1976). A male respondent in Blaxter's study comments: "Men don't go visiting in houses. It's the women who natter over the cups. You wouldn't have men coming here, would you? They'd be awkward. So I do miss my pals" (p. 207).

Blaxter (1976) also reported that the inability to perform certain socially expected roles of daily living, such as keeping a spotless house, preparing food, or serving drinks, sometimes discouraged individuals from taking the initiative to invite friends to their homes. Charmaz (1991) comments about the problem of being homebound:

> Isolation accelerates in old age since many chronically ill elders' social horizons have already shrunk. Unless they possess substantial power, prestige, or property, they cannot bring the outside world into their homes. Even when ill people can bring outsiders in, try as they may, they seldom can keep them coming back beyond the specific task at hand. For example, an elderly man did not leave his home. When he decided to sell his huge library, he cultivated a relationship with the appraiser who also managed the sales. For a few months, the appraiser came in every week or so to pay him and to visit. However, the visits dwindled and ended within a month after they finished their business. (pp. 96-97)

Substitutability of favorite activities is problematic (Iso-Ahola, 1986; Manfredo & Anderson, 1985) and may require professional intervention regarding activity adjustment. Confusion about the abilities of friends with disabilities can produce difficulty in selecting appropriate activities. Ladieu-Leviton et al. (1948), in one of the earliest studies of psychosocial response to disability, found that respondents with disabilities perceived that their nondisabled companions overestimated the physical limitations imposed by the condition, found it difficult to understand that participation could be enjoyed in different roles such as spectator and coach instead of player, and lacked patience with participation that occurred at reduced speed.

Relationship maintenance through the experience of illness and disability may be influenced by the partners' abilities to adjust companionate activity. Successful activity adjustments will be determined jointly by the desire and competence to readjust dyadic activities to accommodate the disability as well as the social and physical accessibility of opportunities for meaningful and enjoyable companionate activity.

Social Support

How does social support change as a result of illness? The 150 respondents in Lyons's (1986) study were asked about changes in the provision and receipt of support as a result of their disability. Sixteen percent indicated that little had changed with respect to the amount and nature of support given to others, 23% reported a decrease in help given to others, and 22% described a change from provision of physical or material aid to an emphasis on the provision of emotional support through verbal communication. Approximately 10% of the respondents indicated that since their condition, they usually were not called on by able-bodied friends to provide support, although another 9% indicated that they placed greater emphasis on helping other people with a disability than prior to onset (i.e., peer support).

Respondents were asked what contributions they perceived they could make to friendships. Close to 10% responded that they had little or nothing to offer others in a relationship, but most respondents outlined contributions in the form of personal attributes, such as listening skills. Other contributions included a particular resource such as motorcycle repair, baking, knowledge, or material possessions. One respondent had constructed a swimming pool in his backyard to attract friends and neighbors and to reciprocate for help received.

Whereas 23% of respondents reported that they received the same amount and type of support from friends since their condition began, 21% said they received more help, and 19% felt that increased emotional support was given to assist them in adjusting to their illness. Several (13%) stated that they now received less, little, or no help from friends. Anecdotal comments from these respondents indicated an exchange style termed *perceived resource deficiency*, the perception that they had little to offer others in a relationship and therefore were unattractive as friends/partners. As one person said, "Lots of money, lots of friends. No money, no friends" (male, 62, stroke) (Lyons, 1991, p. 86).

Also presented was a stoic exchange style, the necessity of depending on oneself when times are tough, and deciding not to involve others as support providers. In general, those with spinal injuries tended to give more positive comments about aid provided by friends than did the stroke or MS group, many of whom expressed resentment about friends deserting them when they were needed. The differences may be attributed to the characteristics of spinal injuries (stable, physical disability) as compared to strokes (cognitive difficulties) and MS (degenerative, multiple symptoms) (Lyons, 1986, 1991).

❧ Relationship Quality

Are people with disabling health problems satisfied with their relationships? Are relational needs being met? Relational satisfaction or well-being in people with a disability has not been systematically measured. However, there are some limited insights into markers of relationship quality such as loneliness, the value of relationships, relationship functioning, and marital satisfaction.

Loneliness and Disability

Evidence suggests that loneliness is a significant component of the illness experience (Lopata, Heinemann, & Baum, 1982; Rubenstein & Shaver, 1982). Perlman (1982) defines loneliness as the gap between perceived relationship quality and expectations. This gap will widen or narrow with changes in perceived relationship quality or changes in relationship expectations. Lyons (1986) examined the relationship between loneliness and disability in individuals with spinal injuries, multiple sclerosis, and strokes. Loneliness scores were significantly related to degree of disability, life satisfaction, adjustment to disability, place of residence (nursing home vs. private residence), and perceived decrease in the number of close and casual friends. Scores were also significantly related to the presence of some physical symptoms, such as chronic tiredness; bowel/bladder problems; and mobility, fine motor coordination, and eating difficulties.

What relational needs constitute the gap between relationship quality and expectation? In the study by Lyons (1991), companionship (enjoyable activity) was found to be a better predictor of loneliness than social support (help). This may be explained by the fact that respondents had acquired their conditions at least 2 years prior to the study, and their need for emotional and instrumental support may have diminished. As time passes, a perceived lack of opportunities for companionship may be a more salient contributor to loneliness than are support needs; however, this issue requires further study.

There is some evidence suggesting that social adjustment to disability may include accommodation for lowered levels of social interaction (Strauss et al., 1984). An interesting question is whether decreased relational expectations reduce loneliness.

The Value of Relationships

The threat of losing relationships to disability or death may increase the perceived value of existing relationships. There is some anecdotal evidence to suggest that increased value is placed on relationships through the experience of illness (Weinberg & Williams, 1978). An account of this change in values is given by a woman permanently disabled by polio:

> But now, far away from the hospital experience, I can evaluate what I have learned. For it wasn't only suffering; it was also learning through suffering. I know my awareness of people has deepened

and increased and that those who are close to me can count on me
to turn all my mind and heart and attention to their problems. I could
not have done that dashing all over a tennis court. (Henrich &
Kreigel, 1961, p. 19)

Another account by a person with a physical disability concludes:
"I have a sharper appreciation of things I valued before—health,
happiness, comfort, friendships. . . . I feel lucky for just being
here" (Dembo, Leviton, & Wright, 1975, p. 57).

Assessment of Relationship Functioning

One area of investigation that relates to quality has involved
markers of marital or family functioning with the presence of
illness. Investigators have noted a variety of effects of chronic
illness on family relationships, including alteration of traditional
family roles and increased psychological distress (Turk, Rudy, &
Flor, 1985). For instance, chronic pain produces deleterious effects
on marital and sexual functioning, increased depression, and psychosocial disorders among spouses (Flor, Turk, & Scholz, 1987;
Kerns & Turk, 1985).

With respect to family functioning and illness, Dura and Beck
(1988) conducted a comparative study of functioning in families
where mothers were experiencing chronic pain, diabetes, and no
illness. Data were collected on parents and children. Families with
a mother who had chronic pain had poorer perceived family
environments (less cohesive and expressive and more controlling
and conflictual) and higher levels of anxiety and depression when
compared to the other two groups. Although research studies
have shown adverse effects of a husband's illness on the wife, this
study showed similar effects on men when their wives had a
chronic illness. Level of disability appeared more a salient factor
than did type of illness in producing family difficulties.

Marital Satisfaction

Several investigations have addressed the relationship between
disability and marital satisfaction. Simmons and Ball (1984) found

that couples in which the male partner had a spinal cord injury reported greater marital satisfaction if they married after rather than before disability onset. Similar findings were reported by Crewe, Athelstan, and Krumberger (1979). Although both groups were similar with respect to disability status, couples married after the onset of disability were not required to adjust or accommodate relational patterns. Individual differences in willingness to assume a high level of caretaking responsibility may also contribute to the higher levels of marital satisfaction in postinjury marriages.

One of the findings that has emerged from this literature is that couples in which one partner has a spinal cord injury frequently report higher marital satisfaction than normative samples (Crewe et al., 1979; Simmons & Ball, 1984). Interpretation of this finding must proceed with consideration of sampling biases present in cross-sectional correlation studies of marital satisfaction. Marital satisfaction can be examined only in couples who are still married. Given the higher rates of divorce in disabled couples, the more dysfunctional couples may not be available for study; examination of the couples who are still married may present an overly optimistic and inaccurate view of how disability influences marital relationships.

In samples of chronic pain patients, disability has been associated with greater marital distress (Flor, Turk, et al., 1987). Factors such as role tension, decreased sexual satisfaction, and increased emotional distress in the nondisabled spouse have been discussed as contributing to marital dissatisfaction (Ahern, Adams, & Follick, 1985; Flor, Turk, et al., 1987). Maruta, Osbourne, Swanson, and Halling (1981) reported that 60% of their sample of chronic pain patients were dissatisfied with the quality of their sexual relations. More than 80% of patients reported a decrease in the frequency of sexual activity following the onset of chronic pain, with as many as 40% reporting complete cessation of sexual activity (Flor, Kerns, et al., 1987; Maruta et al., 1981). Two thirds of pain patients report that their marital relationship has been negatively affected by their illness (Flor, Turk, et al., 1987).

Research has found that solicitous behavior of the nondisabled spouse contributes to higher levels of marital satisfaction reported by the disabled partner, but not marital satisfaction reported by the spouse (Flor, Kerns, et al., 1987). Although reinforcement behaviors were unrelated to marital satisfaction, spouses who engaged in high levels of solicitous behaviors also reported more positive moods and greater control over their lives.

Our knowledge about the quality of relationships and how this changes as a result of disability is still relatively limited. Social networks and frequency of social contact tend to reduce, which may contribute to social isolation and loneliness. However, one must not assume a correlation between network structure and network satisfaction. Smaller networks with less contact may be more manageable for the person with a disabling health problem, although there has been little attention devoted to comparing network structure and relationship quality. There has also been very little comparative work across disabilities or with nondisabled populations; or, as mentioned earlier, on how these structural changes compare with social network changes in other life events such as widowhood or divorce. With respect to communication and activity, there are difficulties maintaining relationships, particularly friendships based on mutually shared activities. If readjustment of companionate activity does not occur, friendship dissolution may.

In marital relationships, we still know little about how changing roles because of disability affect relationships, as well as the role of exchange and equity processes. Obviously, more process research is required. Important but as yet undeveloped topics include issues of love, commitment, and attributions for relationship change. It would be useful to increase research efforts that clarify relational satisfactions and salient needs in relationships where at least one partner has disabling health problems. Obviously, attention to such issues also has been neglected in interventions. Emotional distress resulting from a serious health problem may be related to relational dissatisfaction and distress. If relationships are presumed to deteriorate or decline with a health problem, few resources may be mobilized by partners or health professionals to retain them. Relational commitment and competence in making relationship adjustments are discussed in Chapter 5.

Relationship Roles and Rules

Societal norms about the roles and rules of relationships may influence their maintenance following disability. Interpersonal discomfort with respect to disability may be perceived as reason for avoidance. However, the tendency toward avoidance may be outweighed by affection and social responsibility. This may be particularly true for people who deem that there are social rules in the face of illness and disability that guide them to provide support and to help out, and that strive to make friends and family happy (Argyle & Henderson, 1984). Friendship expectations or roles have been measured by generalized responses to systematic listings of dimensions or informal rules of friendship (Argyle & Henderson, 1984; La Gaipa, 1977), and they also have been assessed in terms of our "real-life" friendships (Shulman, 1975)— why we maintain the friends we do. Research on the retained and lapsed relationships of people with disabling health problems would enhance our understanding about whether an informal set of rules actually exists to guide relationships through disability.

4

The Impact of Relationships on Coping and Adaptation

Question: What is good about your closest relationships?

Reply: Support. You've got someone that supports you. Like the people closest to me are my husband and daughter . . . my husband because he supports me and doesn't try to hold me back. And my daughter because she gives me a reason to want to go on. (p. 76)

If you don't have someone you can ask to do things, then I think what happens is . . . you're swamped. Because you're trying to keep a positive outlook for the family, for the people that you know. And if you've got frustration building up inside you because you can't do things, then that frustration vents itself on the people that you don't want to be on the other end of it. You want them to see you as someone who can deal with things. And I think just having someone help you gives you that strength . . . you can actually go ahead and deal with things. (p. 77)

(Accounts from focus group research
on mothers with multiple sclerosis)
(Meade, 1994)

In recent years, increased attention has been drawn to the role of interpersonal or social support variables in the process of adaptation to chronic illness (Burman & Margolin, 1992; Coyne & Downey, 1991). The benefits of social support in terms of well-being, adaptation to illness, and health outcomes have been widely investigated (e.g., Braverman, 1983; Broadhead et al., 1983; Cohen & Wills, 1985; Hammer, 1983; Lin, Ensel, Simeone, & Kuo, 1979; Lynch, 1977; Nuckolls, Cassel, & Kaplan, 1972; Power, 1985). Supportive behaviors, such as attention and encouragement, can play a role in decreasing suffering, facilitating adaptation to illness and disability, and increasing adherence to treatment and rehabilitation (Meichenbaum & Turk, 1987; Wortman & Conway, 1985). Requesting and accepting aid can also exert positive effects on the maintenance and growth of relationships (Rodin, 1982). Helping behaviors may facilitate social interaction, and in the course of this action may bring participants closer (Heusemann & Levinger, 1976). A national (U.S.) survey of males with disabilities (Smith, 1980) found that social support from family and friends was more highly correlated with adjustment to illness than that provided by the formal health care system.

✥ Social Support Needs

Support needs are defined as the discrepancy between the support required to deal with the stressors of illness and the presence of that support. Support needs can be derived from gaps in sources and types of support pertaining to specific stressors as well as from the appraisal of stressful social interaction (e.g., miscarried helping, conflict). Social support researchers and theoreticians have used various taxonomies to identify social support needs or provisions (e.g., Barr, 1993; Cutrona & Russell, 1987; Gottlieb & Wagner, 1991; Meade, 1994; Stewart, 1993; Weiss, 1974). In the case of a disabling health problem, domains of support need can include the following:

1. *Emotional support*—communication of positive regard, social validation, understanding, and empathy. In a recent study of social support

and adjustment to breast cancer, Hegelson (1994) found that comfort in discussing the illness was a salient support need yet one of the least available types of support.

2. *Informational support*—illness information on diagnosis, treatment and rehabilitation, symptom management, coping strategies, decision-making guidance, and location of resources.

3. *Instrumental aid/practical support*—assistance with basic self-mainte-nance (feeding, dressing, toileting, bathing); care for children; house-hold chores; lodging; treatment and rehabilitation; assistance in work and leisure activity; transportation; financial support; hospital visitation; safety/protection equipment; and the procurement of health, legal, and social services.

From an interdependence perspective, where illness is concep-tualized as a stressor for many personal network members, social support must be defined as efforts aimed at addressing support needs of several parties (Coyne, Ellard, & Smith, 1990). These parties may include spouses or partners, children, parents, and friends. All parties involved—those with an illness and those with whom they have close relationships—potentially provide support within the personal network. Coyne and Fiske (1992) have studied coping and support in the context of couples addressing problems of illness following myocardial infarction. They state:

> In our focus group discussions with post-infarction couples, it was obvious that wives were not simply support people. Their hus-band's health problems had direct implications for their own well-being and they were faced with their own coping tasks. (p. 132)

If we are to assume a communal or relationship approach to coping and support processes in illness, we must ask: What is it that people with disabling health problems and their significant others need from each other to facilitate coping and adaptation? Obviously, support needs vary according to the nature of the condition, symptoms, and course of the condition, as well as the emotional response to that condition.

Family members and close friends may require emotional support to deal with the psychological impact of serious illness in a loved one and social validation for assuming caregiving roles; information about the condition, including symptoms, prognosis, treatment, and rehabilitation; competencies in providing care; and *instrumental help* (e.g., adaptational strategies for addressing such issues as intimacy, household tasks, leisure and finances, respite from caregiving responsibilities, and the fair distribution of caregiving responsibilities among the network and health care workers) (Stewart, 1993).

Determinants of Social Support Provision

What are the factors that influence the provision of social support in chronic illness/disability? Sarason, Pierce, and Sarason (1990) identified three sets of factors that influence support provision: situational, intraindividual, and interpersonal factors. We provide illness-related examples for each of these three sets of social support factors: symptom visibility and social stigma (situational/ illness factors), stress appraisal and gender (intraindividual factors), and relationship functioning in marriage and friendship (interpersonal factors).

Situational Factors—The Nature of the Illness/Disability

In the case of chronic illness, social support provision may be influenced by several illness/disability characteristics, such as diagnosis, the nature and course of symptoms, and treatment and hospitalization. Two of these characteristics are whether the condition/disability is visible, and the degree of stigma attached to particular types of illnesses or symptoms.

Visibility of a stressor such as illness will remind significant others of the health problem and the possible need for support (Fontana, Kerns, Rosenburg, & Colonese, 1989). A disability that is invisible does not immediately cue people to the possibility of support needs or activity adaptations. Mickelson (1993), in a review of research on visibility and social support in cancer and chronic pain patients, suggests that both perceived availability of support and support satisfaction are higher with visible stressors than with those that are not recognizable.

How does a person with an invisible disability broach the subject in social situations? One of the authors received a letter from a man with a weak right hand, due to a mild case of cerebral palsy at birth. He complained of having felt chronically awkward and embarrassed in social situations throughout adulthood because of this handicapping condition. In Britain, a firm handshake and eye contact are important self-presentations in the process of making formal introductions. Feeling self-conscious about his hand and not knowing how to alert others to the need for a handshake "adaptation," he would avert his gaze and lose what he felt was a strategic determinant of acquaintance formation.

Another situational factor is the relationship between stigma associated with a health problem and social support. Stressors related to stigma may include disgrace or shame (AIDS and venereal disease); personal responsibility for the illness or disability (head injury from a car accident caused by drinking and driving); or fears, such as the condition being contagious. Research has shown that the extent of illness or disability is related to social support from family and friends, with the more severe disability associated with less social support and greater difficulty in social interaction (Kiecolt-Glaser, Dyer, & Shuttleworth, 1988; Mickelson, 1993; Turner, Hayes, & Coates, 1993; Wolcott, Namir, Fawzy, Gottlieb, & Mitsuyasu, 1986).

Intraindividual Factors in Social Support

In earlier chapters, the concept of communal processes was introduced as useful in understanding the stress of illness, coping, and adaptation. Now, the notion of communal coping orientation is explored in the context of social support. All social support processes can be considered to contain a social or relationship orientation to coping with a stressor such as illness. However, for some individuals, relationships and social networks are more communally oriented than for others.

Communal coping orientation refers to the extent to which a stressor is viewed in the context of close relationships; in other words, perceiving the issue as "our" problem versus "my" or "your" problem. People with a communal coping orientation toward illness expect that many of the coping *and* support issues will be addressed communally rather than individually. The issues would be shared to a greater extent than would occur with an individual coping orientation (Lyons & Meade, 1993a; Lyons & Mickelson, 1994).

How might a communal coping orientation influence social support? On the positive side, we might speculate that the stress of a disabling health problem is reduced by sharing the responsibility for dealing with it. In networks that are communally oriented toward stressors such as illness, family and friends are *expected* to help out during tough times. They develop a history of support provision, and there is less ambiguity around support roles. Because ill people with a communal coping orientation are concerned about the welfare of others dealing with the presence of the illness, they may be less self-involved with their illness. On the negative side, viewing a stressor communally may lead to higher expectations from one's social network and therefore to a greater chance of disappointment. A person may expect more from network members than members are prepared to give. Correspondingly, there is some research evidence to suggest that higher support expectations are associated with less satisfaction (Bar-Tal, Zohar, Greenberg, & Hermon, 1977; Lam & Power, 1991).

Caring roles of all types traditionally have been the province of women (Henderson & Allen, 1990; Ruddick, 1989). Gilligan (1982) used the term *ethic of care* to suggest that taking care of others, ensuring the well-being of others, and defining oneself in relation to others have been central to the socialization and psychological development of women. Wheaton (1990) suggests that context dependence is, for women, a key factor in the meaning and effects of life events. As stated earlier, the burden of illness often falls on women, whether or not they themselves have the condition (Coyne & Fiske, 1992). In a study of couples coping with myocardial infarction, women tended to resume work and family roles more quickly and felt guilty about changes in household responsibilities (Coyne & Fiske, 1992); men do not report such guilt (Hamilton, 1990). Husbands will hire a housekeeper to take over an ill wife's roles, but a wife is more likely to assume her husband's duties herself (Zarit, Todd, & Zarit, 1986).

Women also have been traditionally responsible for relational maintenance, and they seem to attach more importance to relationship quality. Therefore, if the well-being of women is based more strongly on the perceived well-being of significant others (Brown & Harris, 1978; Gore & Colton, 1991; Gottlieb & Wagner, 1991; Gottman, 1991; Wheaton, 1990), coping with illness may involve attending to how children, parents, and partners are dealing with the illness versus focusing on their own welfare (pain, prognosis, etc.). Men may focus more directly on their own personal loss (e.g., work role, physical attractiveness). Thoits (1991) comments on the salience of relationship stressors such as illness for women:

> The most potent stressors involve losses, disruptions, or conflicts with significant others because these interpersonal breaches threaten the ties that are the primary basis for women's judgements of their own adequacy, that is, for their self-esteem and identity. (p. 150)

In a study of work and leisure constraints in women with disabilities, Henderson, Bedini, and Schuler (1993) found that illness exacerbated preexisting gender inequities regarding distribution of work and family roles. In support of this finding, the following account was one of several in a study of mothers and multiple sclerosis (Lyons & Meade, 1993b), where the attribution of perceived gender inequity contributed to the stresses of illness:

> They say, men don't do. Even if the wife is healthy, the men don't do the housework. They don't contribute as much. It's still the woman that's doing everything. They're the ones that have to go out and work and come home and cater to, you know, try to be there for everybody else. And I know, my husband said something to me one day this year that took all the guilt off me. We said we'd like to have more money. And he said that he didn't want to work two jobs. And I said: "Fine, I don't want to work two jobs, either, but that's what women are doing." It's hard on healthy women and it's even harder for women with health problems. (p. 35)

As women have been socialized into caregiving roles, they have developed expertise in dealing with stressors such as illness. Although women may wish to relinquish some of their caregiving responsibilities, they, and men themselves, may believe that men are not particularly competent in social support provision in response to disabling health problems. Anecdotally, we provide a few comments from a focus group study on women with MS regarding the ability of their husbands to provide support:

> He's not the most understanding person. He doesn't know how to deal with it (the MS) anymore than what he has (diabetes). (Meade, 1994, p. 76)

> Men just don't understand or listen to a lot of emotional problems. They don't want to know. . . . Just ignore it and it will go away. (Meade, 1994, p. 87)

Interpersonal (Relationship) Factors

Several social support researchers (e.g., Dunkel-Schetter & Skokan, 1990; Hansson, Jones, & Fletcher, 1990; Sarason et al., 1990) have emphasized the interpersonal context of social support. There is growing recognition of the importance of the qualitative features of relationships and the social network in social support provision. Such features include the presence of a friendship network, marital quality, and how people relate to each other in times of stress.

Friendship and Social Support. Friendship plays several unique roles in an individual's adjustment to life with a disability. From early childhood, peers perform vital cognitive and emotional developmental functions of social validation and support. Although the nature and structure of friendships vary greatly across the life span (Bigelow & LaGaipa, 1975), the common thread of friendship is voluntary (Hays, 1988).

/To be seen as someone worthy of friendship enhances self-esteem and increases one's psychological resources for dealing with life stressors (Rook, 1987). On the other hand, it has been argued (Babchuk, 1965; Morgan, 1987; Palisi & Ransford, 1987; Rodin, 1982) that the volitional character of friendships provides a ticket to dissolve them if significant gaps persist between expectations and actualities. Social bonds through kin or work may be maintained because of family obligations or financial need, but freedom of choice in friendships provides a special status for their continuation through illness.

With respect to disability, French (1984) has noted that the voluntary nature of a friendship may be perceived as an indication of true caring, whereas family, coworkers, and professionals are under greater obligation to provide support. A study of adjustment to widowhood by Morgan (1987) also showed that relationships with friends had a stronger impact than relationships with family.

People will often turn to friends for emotional support because friends are not bound up in the day-to-day family issues of finance, personal care, and so on. Without such constraints, friends may feel freer to engage in frank dialogue. For instance, anecdotal accounts from disabled people indicate that friends cajole them into getting out of bed and getting on with living as compared with more palliative, less effective approaches from family and health professionals.

Friendships are formed primarily for sociability and mutual enjoyment (Fischer, 1982). If, as Treischmann (1974) has observed, "the key to coping with one's disability is to perceive enough satisfaction and rewards to make life worthwhile" (p. 558), then the pleasure of companionate activity can provide a motive for getting on with life. Enjoyment also diverts attention away from illness and the self-involvement it promotes. A respondent with multiple sclerosis comments: "The babysitter comes for three hours. I get out. Well, I don't do anything. All I do is go with my friend. And we'll sit there. Have a coffee and some calories and relax" (Meade, 1994, p. 85).

Although friends may be important as social support providers, how do they fare in actually meeting the needs of people with disabilities? In a study of 150 adults with spinal injuries, strokes, and multiple sclerosis, respondents were asked by way of an

open-ended question how friends had influenced their adjustment to their health problems (Lyons, 1986, 1991). Positive influences on adjustment were attributed to inclusion in companionate
activity, provision of instrumental and emotional support, and
relational competence around the disability. Negative influences
(behaviors of friends that inhibited adjustment) were primarily
attributed to perceived exclusion from companionate activity and
lack of commitment to the relationship. Interestingly, 30% of respondents gave only negative comments.

The role that friends play in providing social support is not
widely recognized by health professionals. Sourkes (1982) has
reported that relationships that do not fit into a clear category of
"family" are often overlooked by the health care system. Typically,
friends are left out of discussions about patients' health problems
and treatment plans and do not receive information about their
emotional status. Thus, their ability to provide effective support
may be significantly reduced. This lack of knowledge places friends
in a potentially embarrassing situation by not having enough
information to act appropriately.

Another constraint to social support provision by friends may
be family. In a study of cancer and social relationships, LaGaipa
(1984) has noted that friends also may be discouraged from providing support by family members who feel that it is their role to
assume total responsibility for help-giving. Thus, although a friend
may be closer to the patient than any relative, that individual may
not necessarily be accorded this recognition.

Marriage and Social Support. How does involvement in a marital
relationship and the quality of that marital relationship affect
illness/disability? Sullivan, Mikail, et al. (1992) compared the
emotional functioning of married and nonmarried individuals
shortly following diagnosis of MS. Marital status at the time of
diagnosis had little impact on any of the outcome variables. However, in the subsample of people who were married, marital quality was significantly related to adjustment to illness. Individuals
who reported marital difficulties prior to the diagnosis of MS
reported higher levels of depressive symptomatology than did

individuals who did not report previous marital difficulties. Individuals with previous marital difficulties also reported that the illness had been a greater strain on their marriage, and they currently described their partner as being more critical and less supportive. Marital difficulties appeared to exacerbate the stress of illness onset.

Studies that have been conducted on marital quality and coping with mental illness are suggestive of the important role of marital functioning in illness adaptation and recovery. High levels of marital conflict predict relapse in a number of psychiatric disorders, including schizophrenia (Vaughn & Leff, 1976; Vaughn, Snyder, Freeman, Jones, & Faloon, 1984), mania (Miklowitz, Goldstein, Nuechterlein, Snyder, & Mintz, 1988), and major depression (Hooley, Orley, & Teasdale, 1986; Hooley & Teasdale, 1989). These studies have shown that patients living with relatives who are critical or hostile relapsed at a significantly higher rate than did patients living with relatives who were not critical or hostile. In one study, successfully treated depressed patients returning home to highly critical relatives had a relapse rate of 67% within 9 months of discharge compared to 22% of patients with noncritical relatives (Leff & Vaughn, 1980). Hooley and Teasdale (1989) reported that patients' scores on a measure of marital dysfunction predicted relapse as well as spouses' critical expression during an interview-based assessment. The single best predictor of relapse was patients' responses to the question, "How critical is your spouse of you?", accounting for 38% of the variance in patient outcome. Patients who rated their spouse as highly critical (e.g., greater than 6 on a 10-point scale), had a relapse rate of 100% within 9 months of discharge. Patients who rated their spouse as being noncritical (e.g., less than 2 on a 10-point scale) had a 0% relapse rate 9 months postdischarge.

✷ Relationship Issues
in the Provision of Effective Support

Social support is not globally associated with positive outcomes. There may be negative implications of social support for the recipient. These include loss of personal control; dependence; social comparison with other, "more able" people; and the perceived display of personal weakness (Hansson, Jones, & Carpenter, 1984). Fisher and Nadler (1974), among others, have presented the darker sides of receipt of aid on the self-esteem of recipients. Identity as an "impaired" person is often perceived as the cost of disclosure of the need for help. On the donor side, caregivers may be burdened by the overprovision of aid to others. Individuals may feel trapped and unable to escape from a consuming list of emotional and instrumental support requirements. Also, good donor intentions may misfire through provision of support that is misinterpreted or inappropriate.

Support provision that appears helpful when viewed independently can be *counterproductive when viewed interdependently*. What may seem trivial and insignificant to the person without the health problem may be significant and profoundly symbolic to the person with the disabling health problem. For example, a prescribed exercise or diet regimen for health maintenance may seem insignificant to one partner, and of great importance to the other. In the frequently ambiguous role of the supporter, a companion may insist on compliance with the recommended regimen when it has been temporarily or permanently rejected by the individual with the health problem.

Viney (1989) suggests that miscommunication about these concerns is a more salient issue for people with a disabling health problem than for others, because there is a greater dependency on others to validate their personal construct systems. Therefore, oversensitivity in the individual with the health problem and lack of sensitivity to boundary issues by the companion result in a mismatch of support provision with support need. Because of this mismatch, good intentions lead to poor results.

Overprotection

In the personal relationships literature, it has been observed that overinvolvement of the helper may affect the recipient's life as negatively as the underinvolvement of the helper (Coyne,

Wortman, & Lehman, 1988; Gottlieb,1988). In the family interaction literature, the notion of over- and underinvolvement is analogous to the constructs of enmeshment and disengagement (Hoffman, 1975; Minuchin, 1974; Olson, Sprenkle, & Russell, 1979). For example, the Circumplex Model of Family Interaction (CMFI) (Olson et al., 1983) posits that the extremes of excessive cohesion (enmeshment) and deficient cohesion (disengagement or isolation) in family-oriented and intimate interactions are maladaptive.

Overidentification with a chronically ill person can involve the caregiver taking responsibility for the partner's well-being (Coyne & Anderson, 1989). Such exaggerated assumptions of responsibility can lead to unrealistic efforts to "make things right" and disappointments when the recipient does not respond with improvement. In one study, individuals who responded to a distressed confederate (i.e., actor) mainly by supportive listening were significantly less depressed themselves after the interaction than were helpers who provided advice or attempted to distract the confederate from focusing on the dysphoric mood (Notarius & Herrick, 1988). Furthermore, the latter helpers, who were more depressed after the failed helping encounter, were more negative than were the supportive listeners about interacting with the depressed confederate in a variety of future hypothetical situations. This research indicates that more modest attempts at helping and more modest expectations for success may protect the helper from debilitating disappointment while ensuring more consistent support for the recipient.

An overly high investment of the helper in the outcome of helping efforts may even lead to a view that the recipient's continued displays of distress are an implicit accusation that the support offered is inadequate (Bullock, Siegal, Weissman, & Paykel, 1972). The helper may personalize the situation and polarize against the recipient. This has been termed characterological attack and rejection (Coyne et al., 1988).

A fundamental irony in the dynamics of social support may be that the very emotional bonding that sustains supportive relationships also makes them more vulnerable to emotional excesses during crises or periods of distress. This vulnerability to emotional overinvolvement in support relationships may necessitate professional counseling, where detachment from day-to-day life curbs emotional reactivity on the therapist's part. In any case, it is evident that an effective support relationship requires a cognitive-affective balance in the helper so that the *needs* of the recipient can be sensitively addressed.

There is another side to the issue of overprotection. Discussions of overprotectiveness usually have been couched within theoretical frameworks that have emphasized the destructive nature of overprotective behavior (Levy, 1943). Overprotectiveness has been viewed as the expression of excessively nurturant or caring behavior driven by unconscious hostile motives (Levy, 1943). More recent conceptualizations have emphasized the need to distinguish between nurturant behavior and hostile motives in responses to disability (Fiske et al., 1991).

A number of investigators have recently discussed overprotectiveness as a normative and even adaptive response to disability (Fiske et al., 1991; Gillis, 1984). Overprotectiveness may facilitate recovery by reducing the stress of disability, and it may communicate caring and support to the individual with the disabling health problem. Indeed, there are indications that overprotectiveness following chronic illness and disability may increase emotional closeness within the marital relationship (Fiske et al., 1991). In the case of myocardial infarction, it has been suggested that overprotectiveness may represent spouses' attempts to reduce the likelihood of losing a close relationship (Fiske et al., 1991).

There are indications that for individuals with chronic pain, overprotective or solicitous behaviors by the spouse may reinforce disability behavior and contribute to greater functional impairment. Research in this area has been prompted by theoretical perspectives emphasizing that the expression of disability behavior, although initially determined by symptom levels, can come under the control of external reinforcement contingencies (Fordyce, 1976). Within this conceptualization, conditioning processes related to the reinforcing properties of attention from the spouse, escape from unpleasant responsibilities, and lack of reinforcement of "well behaviors" are considered to be significant determinants of disability behavior independent of symptom levels.

The substantive role of the spouse in determining the expression of disability behavior in chronic pain has been demonstrated in several investigations. For example, Block, Kremer, and Gaylor (1980) reported that pain patients' level of pain expression varied as a function of whether they were told they were being observed by their spouse or by a ward clerk. Patients whose spouses were identified as solicitous (i.e., attentive) rated their pain levels as higher when they thought they were being observed by their spouses as opposed to a ward clerk. Patients whose spouses were identified as nonsolicitous (i.e., spouses who ignored pain behaviors) rated their pain lower when they thought they were being observed by their spouses as opposed to a ward clerk.

Similar findings were reported by Flor, Kerns, and Turk (1987) in an observational field study of pain patients interacting with their spouses. Spouses' self-reported reinforcement behaviors were found to be the best single predictor of patients' pain and activity level. Reinforcement behaviors by the spouse were associated with increased pain complaints and decreased activity.

Observational research has yielded similar findings (Romano et al., 1991). The results of sequential analyses revealed that solicitous behaviors functioned as discriminative cues for the expression of pain behaviors, and pain behaviors functioned as negative reinforcers of spousal aggression (Romano et al., 1991). In other words, solicitous behavior by the spouse increased the probability of verbal and nonverbal expressions of distress by the chronic pain patient, and the expression of pain behavior decreased the probability of the expression of verbal aggression by the spouse.

Caregiving

Family caregiving to an individual with a disabling health problem can involve considerable role adaptation. The extent of the role change varies considerably depending on the illness and the presence of formal (health care workers) and informal (family and friends) supports. Mingo (1993), in her personal account of being a caregiver for her husband with terminal cancer, spent 2 years of her life totally involved in instrumental and emotional support for her husband. She had few social relationships and little social support. She and her husband were recently married and had begun a business. Not only was she faced with the condition itself, but she was forced to seek welfare payments because of full-time caregiving.

The costs of caregiving often include anxiety, strain in performing routine roles, and the need to perform additional roles. Caregivers can feel drained, resentful, and "trapped" (Gottlieb, 1989; Thompson & Doll, 1982). Evans and Northwood (1981), in a study of social support and strokes, reported that the cognitive problems faced by people with a stroke, especially the inability to correctly judge the nature and extent of social support offered, severely interfered with the ability to use that assistance.

On one level, the restrictive side of caregiving is obvious. On another level, caregiving *can* be perceived as an important and valued social role, with special competencies and more personal satisfaction attached to it than to many work roles. However, lack of acknowledgment of supportive behaviors or criticism of support given, as sometimes experienced in stroke, head injury, or Alzheimer's disease patients, will contribute to caregiver distress. There is also reduced support for the caregiver within the relationship because reciprocity is diminished and the care receiver no longer provides support at previous levels.

Response to Caregiver Burden by the Recipient. To reduce the demands of caregiving, the recipient of care may feel pressured to respond with signs of improvement, relieve strain on the caregiver, and reduce the sense of being burdensome. When improvement in health status is impossible, the recipient may adopt a more stoic self-representation as the best possible alternative for reducing caregiver stress (Kramlinger, Swanson, & Maruta, 1983). Thus, the helping relationship may involve purposely "falsified" exchanges that avoid confrontation with the lack of change and prospects for minimal future change.

Further difficulties may arise. For example, when the recipient's self-presentation of improved status or stoicism is a "front" and not a directly experienced reality, he or she can be caught in a dilemma of concealment versus disclosure (Hilbert, 1984). If convincing, the self-presentation sets up in the helper unrealistic assessments of the recipient's condition, leading to subsequent doubts about the authenticity of difficulties when they *are* eventually conveyed by the recipient.

The caregiver must be able to balance the costs of caregiving with social contacts that provide individual stimulation, gratification, and support. Such contacts with individuals who are specifically *not* involved or minimally involved with the stress of the particular caregiving situation may be surprisingly important. These people will be likely to provide more objective appraisals of the situation that are less emotionally dominated, providing a counterbalance to emotional excesses (Cohen & McKay, 1983). These contacts are also the means for the helper to retain an autonomous social existence while being sensitive to the autonomy needs of the recipient (Van Uitert, Eberly, & Engdahl, 1985).

Support Groups and Peers
With Disabling Health Problems

There is evidence to suggest that mutual support and understanding can be gained from relationships with other ill or disabled people (Binger et al., 1969; Bozeman et al., 1955; Dunkel-Schetter & Wortman, 1982). First, there are benefits in observing and identifying with others who can serve as models for successful adjustment. Second, there is a special dynamic that arises when individuals with similar difficult adversities provide mutual aid. The common bond of a similar health problem and the social support benefits of such relationships are identified in the following account by a man with MS from a study on friendship and disability (White, 1994):

> Ironically, the first sales call that I did was on a gentleman with MS. He didn't know that I had it and I didn't know that he had it, other than I noticed a cane in the corner of his office and I noticed his ability to walk was somewhat hampered. I had said to him: "Well, I think we have something more in common than just business." He and I talked quite a bit because I was the first person that he had met with MS. Like, he and I said we'd get together and we got the wives together because my wife had not met anybody to talk about this. (p. 40)

Because individuals in self-help groups confront the aversive disadvantages of illness or disability with a greater sense of mutual identification, compensatory acts of support transcend illness restriction. Other benefits of self-help groups include shared coping strategies, emotional support, exchange of experiential knowledge, and reciprocity.

In summary, close relationships provide both supports and stressors in coping with illness for the person with the condition and for significant others. Chronic illness is so different a state of being. It colors one's perspective so profoundly that people with disabling health problems and those without may have substantially different worldviews. This discrepancy complicates the effective provision and receipt of social support in close relationships. Knowing the nature and extent of support required is difficult to gauge. Although family members may mobilize efforts to assist a disabled individual, miscommunication and overidentification can lead to difficulties in effective support provision. The lack of effective support provision can increase conflict in interpersonal relations. Excessive support provision may also interfere with independence and may even contribute to increased disability behavior.

Beyond family relationships, support groups can play a major role for people with a disabling health problem as well as for caregivers and family members. Also, the role or potential role of existing friendships in support provision should not be ignored. Both support groups and friendships are important in and of themselves, and also in supplementing family support networks. The influence of close relationships on coping is an important yet complex process. If work in this area is to advance, social support models must incorporate the individual, interpersonal, interactional, and temporal factors that are involved in adaptation to disability. Unfortunately, with financial constraints, the health care system has become increasingly reliant on informal supports provided by family and friends. This has occurred without any clear mandate for shoring up the support resources of family and friends.

5

Relationship-Focused Coping

Instead of going apple picking I baked the apple cake and sent it to school, and went in and did a story time about apples. . . . It just takes a whole lot of thinking to try and feel like you're a good mom. I mean you just can't do it the easy way. You have to think it through and think of how you can. . . . Constantly I feel I'm thinking how I can . . . be a good mom with the limitations I'm faced with.

(Lyons & Meade, 1995, p. 197)

It's also hard to deal with when you're talking to a friend . . . a close friend. They ask you how you're doing and you tell them a little bit and you can see them on the verge of tears. . . . "Don't cry, I mean, I'm not dying." . . . You know, it's kind of backward. I want to console them.

(Lyons & Meade, 1995, p. 193)

Coping is not a unified construct. Rather, it is a metaconstruct under which a number of phenomena are embedded (Eckenrode, 1991). Coping generally refers to the strategies that people use to manage and master stressful circumstances and to minimize the negative impact of life stressors on psychological well-being (Lazarus, 1966; Lazarus & Folkman, 1984; Pearlin & Schooler, 1978). According to Lazarus and Folkman (1984), the coping process begins with an appraisal or evaluation of the stressful situation. It is argued that individuals evaluate both the stress properties of the situation (primary appraisal)—in this case, the presence of a disabling health problem—and their ability to deal effectively with such stresses (secondary appraisal). Within this conceptualization, individuals deal with stress by attempting either to change the nature of the stress situation (problem-focused coping) or to manage their emotional reactions to the stress situation (emotion-focused coping).

According to Moos and Tsu (1977), the major sets of adaptive tasks associated with illness include dealing with pain and incapacitation, dealing with the hospital environment, developing adequate relationships with professional staff, preserving a reasonable emotional balance, preserving a satisfactory self-image, preserving relationships with family and friends, and preparing for an uncertain future. Other adaptive tasks in chronic illness and disability would include dealing with financial issues and making lifestyle adaptations in work, leisure, and family activities. (Many of these issues were discussed in Chapter 2.)

Research on coping with illness has proceeded from two major orientations. In one line of research, individuals with disabilities have been asked to endorse items on self-report measures of coping activity. A different approach has been to ask individuals in a more open-ended format about the stresses they have faced and the efforts they have made to overcome these stresses. Gottlieb suggests that people are able to identify the stressors with which they are faced, and the strategies or efforts they mobilize to deal with these stressors, as well as the outcome of their coping efforts:

When we interview people who have been dealing with the repeated demands that characterize these chronic stress contexts, they often comment on the efficacy of their coping efforts. Again, this is without prompting from us. They tell us how they coped, and then they append such comments as: ". . . but it doesn't work," ". . . and that seems to make me feel better," and ". . . that's a better way of handling things between us." . . . These efficacy appraisals are sometimes leveled at the impact of certain ways of coping on the relationship, but also that when people must repeatedly deal with the same stressors, they are more likely to become aware of the responses that do and don't work for them. (Gottlieb, in Lyons, 1993a, p. 13)

In this chapter, we review both quantitative and qualitative research on coping with illness. What is striking about comparing these literatures is that each paints a very different picture of coping with chronic illness. The quantitative literature characterizes the individual in his or her solitary struggle to overcome the limitations of disability with the goal of minimizing the experience of emotional distress. The qualitative literature paints the picture of an individual within a relational environment struggling to maintain functional abilities in order to meet social and relational responsibilities.

Coping and Emotional Distress

Considerable research has examined the relationship between coping and adjustment to disability in people with chronic illness (for reviews, see Devins & Seland, 1987; Jensen, Turner, Romano, & Karoly, 1991). Several studies have shown that individuals with chronic back pain who have coping styles characterized by passivity, avoidance, or excessive negativity show heightened levels of depressive symptomatology (Rosenstiel & Keefe, 1983; Turner & Clancy, 1986). Similar findings have been reported in individuals with MS (Sullivan, Edgley, et al., 1992). In populations without obvious disabilities, individuals experiencing high levels of emotional distress also report using more passive or avoidant strategies than do individuals experiencing low levels of emotional distress (Billings & Moos, 1981, 1984; Coyne, Aldwin, & Lazarus, 1981; Holahan & Moos, 1987). Whereas measures of avoidant coping or escape coping have been consistently associated with increased depressive symptomatology, it has been more difficult to empirically demonstrate that proactive cognitive or behavioral coping strategies are beneficial in dealing with the stresses of chronic illness.

There are also indications that different types of illnesses and disabilities may require different coping skills and strategies. For instance, in the case of heart disease, myocardial infarctions and cardiac arrests have abrupt onsets and usually involve hospitalization, whereas people with ongoing heart disease may require surgery, such as coronary bypass or coronary angioplasty (dilation of coronary arteries). Although both situations may require substantive lifestyle adaptations, surgery involves periods of fear and anxiety (Atkins, Kaplan, & Toshima, 1991). With unpredictable and/or degenerative conditions, such as Parkinson's disease and MS, coping with chronic uncertainty poses other kinds of threats to psychological well-being. In long-term illness or disability, the emphasis is not only on the management of an acute threat, as with a temporary condition, but also the development of new patterns of behavior and the design of new interpersonal roles (Adams & Lindemann, 1974).

Coping profiles may vary across different patient or problem categories that are associated with separate or distinct life stresses such as those given above (Vitaliano et al., 1990). For example, research has shown that individuals with physical illnesses or psychiatric illnesses can be distinguished on the basis of their coping profiles (Vitaliano et al., 1987; Vitaliano et al., 1990). It is assumed that the stresses faced by individuals *within* specific patient or problem categories are sufficiently similar, at least at a conceptual or thematic level, to yield relatively homogeneous coping profiles (Vitaliano et al., 1990).

Sullivan and colleagues compared the coping profiles of individuals with MS and individuals with chronic back pain (Sullivan, Edgley, Mikail, Dehoux, & Fisher, 1992). Results indicated that individuals with MS scored higher on measures of cognitive coping than did individuals with chronic back pain, whereas the two groups did not differ on measures of behavioral coping or avoidant coping. Cognitive coping strategies emphasize different ways of mentally representing disability rather than means of changing the disability. The authors suggested that disability characteristics like mobility restrictions and prognosis may account for the increased cognitive coping observed in the MS sample. Acceptance and attempts to increase understanding about the condition may represent modes of coping best suited to deal with chronic illnesses characterized by progressive deterioration and poor prognosis.

Quantitative approaches have traditionally used emotional distress as a marker for adaptational success. The assumption has been that people who cope better should be less depressed. But if we take a close look at personal accounts of coping, people do not focus exclusively on emotional functioning as the goal of their coping attempts. Personal accounts suggest that people engage in coping strategies to reduce the negative functional impact of disability, enhance the emotional well-being of family members and friends, and maintain their involvement in personal relationships. Our attention on emotional outcome may be diverting our focus away from where coping is having its greatest impact.

❧ Coping With Chronic Illness—The Relationship View

As noted earlier, coping has been traditionally conceptualized as the *individual* pursuit of *self-maintenance* through stress; that is, what did *I* do to deal with the emotional and instrumental stressors of *my* problem? The individualistic approach to coping with illness has been challenged recently in work by several investigators. From research on couples coping with cardiovascular disease, Coyne et al. (1990) suggest that individual models of stress and coping do not adequately account for the relational nature of coping observed in couples and families dealing with health problems. In varying degrees, people not only wish to enhance their own well-being, but the well-being of their families and friends and their relationships. Coyne states:

> People in enduring relationships know that they cannot simply be concerned about the stressor at hand, but need to take into account

the actions of the partner, the relational implications of what they themselves do and the need to preserve the quality and resourcefulness of the relationship. So relationship-focused coping ought to be given the same status as emotion-focused, and problem-focused, although those categories are a lot less tidy in actual application than they first seem. (Coyne, in Lyons, 1993a, p. 12)

Currently, investigators are calling for greater attention to aspects of relational factors in coping with chronic illness. However, there is as yet no comprehensive model that details the stresses, strategies, and outcomes of relationship-focused coping. We believe that a viable conceptual framework of relationship-focused coping should address the following six dimensions: the revaluation of self and relationships, the containment of illness impact on relationships, network remodeling, relationship adaptation, relationship reciprocity, and communal coping.

The Revaluation of Self and Relationships

Reappraisal of self in relationships includes cognitive and emotional strategies to modify expectations of "normative" social role performance. Wright (1983) termed this process *revaluation*—the enlargement and adaptation of one's scope of values. With respect to relationships, this might include changed perspectives about what is important in marriage and friendship. It may also include subordination of physique in relationships (a salient issue in the case of breast cancer or amputations) and positive self-evaluation (reassessing one's worth in positive terms). This type of evaluation also might involve elevating positive aspects of the relationship (e.g., we can't do some things the way we used to do them, but we have other things going for us in our relationship).

The following is an example of revaluation from a woman with MS, with respect to her role as a mother:

You see that you're not as flawed as people make you out to be. That you can still be a woman, you can still be a mother. . . . You know, even with the MS, I know that I'm a good mother. (Lyons & Meade, 1995, p. 195)

The Containment of Illness Impact on Relationships

Containment of disability effects may involve activity adaptations that avoid conflict with disability symptoms, such as the temporal scheduling of events around "healthy" times/remissions, or diverting attention from the centrality of illness in the relationship or social unit. This may proceed through several strategies.

A. Focusing attention on specific, manageable challenges:

Stop worrying about things that you cannot change. . . . And there's other things that you can. . . . If you can change [it], fine, and if you can't, don't dwell on it—you're just wasting energy: energy that we need. (Lyons & Meade, 1995, p. 196)

B. Focusing on the present:

You have to seize . . . especially for a child, the moment. Spend as much time as you can. Because what happens if tomorrow you can't do . . . you can't go for a ride on the swings like you did today, or you could have done today. So you have to make sure you make time for them. (Lyons & Meade, 1995, p. 196)

C. Downplaying illness as a constraint:

I think it's important not to let MS stand in your way. . . . In making friendships, I think, "Oh, I'm different," and I may hold back. . . . Because if it's going to be a friend, they don't care. (Lyons & Meade, 1995, p. 196)

D. Avoidance of illness assuming a dominant place in one's life and one's relationships:

I think it's really easy to become preoccupied. I mean . . . it's not an easy condition. . . . You can spend a lot of time studying how your foot feels today . . . or how you're walking today in comparison with how you did yesterday and looking for. . . . It's like anything, anybody can get caught up in the state of their health. I think what the big thing is . . . is remembering that there are other people there and that they have needs, too. (Lyons & Meade, 1995, pp. 196-197)

E. Maintaining a sense of self-efficacy and control:

> You have to have a fighting spirit. Like, I'm not going to let this control me. I'm going to live, but pace myself. . . . You have your limitations and you understand them. (Lyons & Meade, 1995, p. 196)

Network Remodeling

In Chapter 3, one relationship change that occurred as a result of illness was the intentional termination of relationships and the restructuring of the social network to accommodate the limitations of the health problem. Reduced resources, including energy for socializing, suggest that time must be carefully allocated for relationships. Relationships may be discontinued or reduced in intensity. Reasons for opting out of specific relationships may include decreased physical proximity, nonsupportive or stigmatizing reactions to the illness; or the desire to focus on one's most valued relationships. Also, other people who can provide additional coping resources may be added to the network (e.g., health professionals, individuals with similar health problems, or support groups). Support groups may provide a relaxed, accepting social environment in which members with firsthand experience can address common issues:

> Every time I go to a meeting—our chapter's not very large, there's about a dozen people there—I feel so calm. You know, there's some in wheelchairs, and some like myself, and I thought, "Well, these people are almost . . ." they become really close, these people understand if you trip over something. Someone that doesn't have MS will kind of look at you and just, you feel so uncomfortable. These people understand. (Lyons & Meade, 1995, p. 199)

Relationship Adaptation

The social intrusiveness of illness and disability may require that increased attention be given to strategies that will preserve and maintain the quality of valued relationships. Gottlieb comments on the use of social support seeking as a relationship maintenance strategy:

I began to realize that coping is determined in part by the need to maintain relationships with others—not to alienate them by one's way of coping. The reason for drawing on relationships for support is to shore those relationships up, and the reason for coping in certain ways is to keep important people involved with you or at least to believe that this is the case. (Gottlieb, in Lyons, 1993a, p. 11)

Modification of companionate activity may include activity adaptation and substitution, as well as changes in the location, timing, and intensity of activities. Issues of cooperation, task allocation, and practical support such as transportation or finance also may need to be addressed. The following are examples of how such adaptations occurred in the social network of women with MS.

Companionate Activity Adaptation With Children. Concerns included the maintenance of quality parenting, the adaptation of parent-child activities, and the sharing of household tasks:

But I don't think that you can say you're not a good mother because you can't do certain things. Because you can do others. You can take them to a concert where you can go and sit down for an hour or so and enjoy the concert. You can be the mother that the kids want to come talk to. (Meade, 1994, p. 98)

My little one was four and T. [son] was six and you know . . . [t]he next year come Christmas time, I said to the kids, "Look, it's Christmas for me, too, and I want to enjoy Christmas. And you want me there with you." They scrubbed floors. They learned how to do the wash. They learned how to do everything. And it's been nothing but positive. (Meade, 1994, p. 105)

Companionate Activity Adaptation With Partners. An important consideration may be the increased investment of a partner's efforts on household instrumental tasks to free up energy for relationships:

If I'd had to get all the supper ready and everything, I wouldn't have had the energy to go out and socialize last night. So he . . . by him taking care of the supper, it enabled us to go out. . . . So because he helped, I was able to enjoy the evening and not be too tired. (Lyons & Meade, 1995, p. 198)

Relationship Reciprocity

This dimension of relationship-focused coping involves attention to the (emotional and instrumental) well-being of significant others and of the social unit, and the maintenance of social equity. Although the exchange and equity research typically attends to individuals maximizing or ensuring their own gains, coping is not only tied to self-enhancement but the well-being of family and friends.

> M. had to cancel his sea trip, the whole shebang. Yeah, [my doctor] said there was no way I could be on my own. So . . . it was quite a crisis for us. (Lyons & Meade, 1995, p. 193)

Along with support needs, there is a concern for maintenance of reciprocity and fairness in relationships.

> Well, we actually had kind of an interesting couple of weeks. I started another attack—this hand has gone kind of weird on me. And I wasn't quite over my last attack that I was treated for and I was really down. And at the same time, R. [partner] pulled a muscle in his shoulder and . . . he finally . . . I'm glad he said it. . . . He said, "It seems like your MS is more important than my shoulder." And [I said], "No, that's not the case." But by the time I get in bed at 11 o'clock at night, and he wants me to rub his shoulder, I'm just too tired. . . . And while he understands [that], and he's really very helpful, he was feeling lousy too. . . . But at least he was able to say that. And so, the next night, I made an extra effort. By 8 o'clock, we sat down and actually . . . before I got too tired, and I put some stuff on his shoulder. (Lyons & Meade, 1995, pp. 192-193)

Communal Coping

Many aspects of coping and adaptation may be shared rather than addressed individually. Couples, nuclear or extended family, or close friends may adopt the position that illness is "our problem," and so they cope with many of the emotional (e.g., anger, frustration, disappointment) and instrumental (e.g., income, treatment, child care) aspects of a health problem together (Lyons & Mickelson, 1994). The following account provides an example of the notion of communal coping:

I phoned up my close family and my close friends and thought I may as well do this all at once. So I sat down with Mother Bell just loving it. I did all the phone calls at once, just one after the other. "The good news is I don't have a brain tumor. The bad news is, I have MS. We'll cope with this. You know, in a couple of weeks, two weeks from now, we'll cope with this."

So it gave everybody sort of that time. Certainly it helped them develop the right perspective although none of them had really been aware of the fact that the brain tumor was another option. . . . And everybody did call back in two weeks. After I'd sort of come to grips with it. But you know, I went home and had a good cry—after I did all those phone calls, I had a cry. My husband went and got our kids from day care and by God, those kids wanted dinner, just the same. And I think by giving the people closest to us this two-week hiatus . . . then they don't feel obliged to say too much right away. And a number of them did say, one of my closest friends: "I just don't know what to say to you." "Don't say anything. It's a bitch . . . but better than a brain tumor." (Meade, 1994, pp. 113-114)

In this circumstance, the respondent is describing a coping strategy that has little to do with her own well-being directly. She is concerned with the emotional response of her friends to the diagnosis, and how they will cope with the news of her illness. She develops a strategy to break the news, intending to facilitate their dealing with it and easing their necessity to say the "right" thing to her. Her language also identifies the issue as "our problem" versus "her problem." She has constructed the illness as a network issue, a relationship challenge, rather than isolating herself as the victim. On another note, the explanation of family dinner demands points out the social context within which the illness is being experienced. The intrusiveness of the centrality of illness is diverted in the face of everyday roles and responsibilities.

Another account describes a spouse's use of communal coping to reduce the impact of a diagnosis of MS:

I remember going to my husband's work. I took him aside and asked him to come into the cafeteria with me. And I said, "I have MS." And I still remember, he hugged me and he said, "We'll deal with it together" and boy, did that mean a lot! (Lyons & Meade, 1995, p. 207)

༞ Determinants of Relationship-Focused Coping

The decision to engage in relationship-focused coping is affected by a variety of individual, relational, contextual, and situational factors. For instance, gender is an important factor. There is the belief that women are more competent in dealing with illness than are men, and that dealing with illness in relationships is, in general, more of a women's issue (Gottlieb & Wagner, 1991; Lyons & Meade, 1995). Women who are ill are more concerned about the well-being of others than are men with the same illness, and therefore women will likely place more effort than will men in the construction of coping strategies for the benefit of others, as well as relationships, versus their own needs. Illness also appears to push women toward more conservative gender roles (Lyons & Meade, 1995). However, there are several other factors besides gender in the use of relationship-focused coping strategies, such as commitment and relational competence. In the case of breast cancer, commitment will affect the degree of effort exerted by friends and family members to be supportive or the efforts of a spouse to maintain sexual activity in marriage. Commitment will influence the extent of personal sacrifice for another's well-being. This might even include considerations that may appear to be trivial choices, such as taking time off work for hospital visits or decisions as extensive as giving up paid work to assume caregiving. Relational competence functions might involve discussing the diagnosis with family and friends and sorting out such relational issues as sexuality after surgery.

Commitment

Hinde (1981) defines commitment as "the extent to which the partners in a relationship either accept their relationship as continuing indefinitely or direct their behaviors toward ensuring its continuance or optimizing its properties" (p. 14). Newcomb (1981) identifies two components of commitment: personal commitment (the extent to which one is invested in the relational bond and its continuation) and behavioral commitment (what actions people take to influence longevity in a relationship). As relationships grow and become more valued, commitment and investment progress (Duck & Sants, 1983). Because the onset of a disability typically requires that extra attention be paid to preserve and adapt relationships, the value placed on their continuity will strongly influence the level of behavioral commitment to this end.

Commitment to relationships where one person has a serious health problem may depend on many issues, including the perceived strength of the relationship and the nature of the preillness relationship, the pleasure/cost ratio (Rodin, 1982), relational needs, the degree of social responsibility to help significant others in need, personal climate (i.e., encouragement by others to maintain the relationship), and other social and lifestyle commitments. Behavioral commitment may depend on perceived time availability. Commitment norms are different for parents as compared to couples. Commitment and vigilance were key issues for mothers of chronically ill children (Lyons & Langille, 1995).

It has been suggested that relational bonds are not merely a reflection of prevailing social values (Fisher & Galler, 1988), but constitute a public sphere of their own (Minnich, 1985). However, an interesting question surrounds the comparative influence of contextual factors on relationships versus the influence of partners' or friends' commitment to relationship maintenance itself. This issue may be particularly salient for people with health problems that carry a high degree of stigma. For instance, where there is strong social pressure from family to dissolve a relationship in which one person has AIDS, what degree of relational commitment is required to override such interference?

The concept of social boundaries, used frequently in sociological and anthropological research (Banfield, 1958; Honigmann, 1968; Merton, 1957; Pearlin, 1991), may explain why some companions withdraw from relationships with people with disabilities. Boundaries may be established that provide justification for the termination of relationships with people who become disabled. These may be established so as not to become overcommitted to an overabundance of relationships, all potentially requiring support at some time or another. Attributions may be based on the rationale that the relationship was not particularly close, and therefore little responsibility exists to provide the support required by an acquaintance with health problems or to continue the relationship under new conditions.

Commitment issues may be very different in family versus friend relationships. Compared to family, friends are less bound by societal rules (Sapadin, 1988), and thus, the decision to preserve, adjust, or terminate a friendship lies heavily on the dyad. In essence, the decision to maintain, adjust, or terminate most types of relationships with the onset of disability may be influenced by disability and contextual factors; however, in the end, personal commitment to the relationship will likely make a substantive contribution to the fate of the relationship.

Relational Competence

Hansson et al. (1984) define relational competence as the characteristics that facilitate the acquisition, development, and maintenance of satisfactory relationships. With respect to disability, relational competence to maintain a relationship in the face of illness and disability concerns the ability to address the individual and relational stressors identified throughout this book. Relational competence is likely influenced by socialization experiences with disability or a related situation, as well as personality and social skill.

Strategies to increase relational competence have been addressed anecdotally in the disability literature, with such prescriptions as honest dialogue and discussions about what is helpful and what is not (Cook & Makas, 1979). Charmaz's (1991) single respondents provided a number of strategies for reducing their social isolation, such as hosting potluck dinners, scheduling regular visits and phone checks with friends, and joining a telephone chain group. Other strategies have included the establishment of at least one close friendship with a nondisabled person (Allen, 1976). It has been suggested (Robinson & Thompson, 1980) that one sign of "honest" interaction between disabled and nondisabled people is a disabled person being rejected because of personality as opposed to continuing a false relationship based on the perceived obligation of the disability. However, research that assesses the effectiveness of strategies to enhance relational competence in illness and disability is sorely needed.

Another side of the question relates to the precise matching of behaviors with needs or expectations. People often will avoid interaction with someone with a health problem because they are unsure of the appropriate thing to do or say. Is it all that important to be on target? Relationships operate by particular informal rules governing being there and helping out when needed; however, we may forgive some rule breaking simply because we like them or because they compensate for a deficiency in relational competence by some other strength (Wiseman, 1986). The following account reflects this broader view of acceptable social behavior.

> A good friend at work couldn't bear to come visit me but he wrote the most beautiful letters, even though he was only blocks away. The letters were fantastic. (female, 28, spinal injury) (Lyons, 1986, p. 85)

Expectations of relational competencies may differ based on the nature of the relationship as well as individual personalities. For instance, one may tolerate a communication faux pas or miscarried helping efforts if perceived as a sincere attempt to be helpful, as compared to the same behavior displayed by a friend or family member who is thought to be socially skilled in such circumstances.

The question of how nondisabled people become relationally competent must extend beyond "helping" skills to everyday communication and companionate activity. The problems identified under "companionate activities" indicate that activity adjustment is a form of relational competence salient for the maintenance of friendships. In the end, we may need to be more willing to take "relational risks" to socially integrate people with disabilities. People with disabilities also may need to become more aware of relational processes not only to correctly perceive social behaviors but also to exert greater control over their social networks and personal relationships.

In this chapter, we have examined coping and adjustment processes and their determinants, suggesting that coping is a process that involves the individual with the condition and significant others and is conducted in the context of personal relationships. We are only beginning to gain insight into specific relationship-focused coping strategies that people use to deal with illness and the strategies that are beneficial over the long run. An area in need of further study is the efficacy of methods to share useful coping strategies. How can individuals with a health problem and their significant others most effectively gain knowledge of coping and adaptational strategies? What methods are currently used—health professional's, friend's, or family member's advice; role modeling of family members or others with a health problem; experiential knowledge; self-help groups; or books? What are effective venues for acquiring coping and adaptational skills?

It is intuitively appealing to maintain high regard for the power of individualistic coping efforts in dealing with significant life stress. Adding relationship-focused coping may broaden the predictive value of coping. Pearlin (1991) has cautioned against a microview that excludes the influential roles of contextual factors such as social conditions and policies. In a sense, how a society copes with illness and disability should be factored into any examination of coping for individuals and their relationships. New models of coping that address how the stress of illness and disability is managed and mastered should contain several levels of coping efforts, from societal to individual. They should also contain the intended purpose or functions of coping strategies, including those that maintain and enhance close relationships.

6

Intervention in
Close Relationships
to Improve Coping With Illness

James C. Coyne

Expanding interest in the study of close relationships as the context of illness and disability has coincided with a greater appreciation of the possibilities of intervening in these relationships as a way of improving physical health and psychosocial outcomes. Yet these developments have been independent rather than synergistic. The classic split between researchers and clinicians and the rarity of the researcher-clinician is as pronounced in the domain of close relationships and health as anywhere. Researchers pay little attention to whether their key hypotheses, methods, and variables have any correspondence to the practical concerns of clinicians. Therapists and other health professionals working to improve couples' coping with illness take little counsel from researchers. Psychological researchers aspire to publish their best studies of couples and health in *Journal of Personality and Social Psychology* or *Journal of Consulting and Clinical Psychology*, where they are unlikely to be seen by relationship-oriented clinicians. In turn, these clinicians tend to look to *Family Process* and *Family Systems Medicine* for guidance in dealing with health issues. If researchers have even heard of these journals, they are unlikely to peruse them on a regular basis.

This volume represents an effort to bridge this unfortunate gulf, but in attempting to do so, we must confront basic differences in culture as well as language. In this chapter, we make the transition to intervention and we hope that no one is lost in the passage. It is our strong sense that not only do the researcher and clinician have much to offer each other, but each has something to gain in the process of simply articulating what they do so that the other can understand. Researchers stand to become more sensitive to the issues and concerns actually faced by people coping with illness and the challenges facing professionals trying to effect change in how they cope. Clinicians could benefit from having to phrase their hypotheses in more testable terms and from accepting that claims of effectiveness must ultimately be backed by data.

At the outset, it should be noted that data concerning the efficacy of intervention in close relationships to improve health outcomes are quite limited, and general arguments for such interventions cannot yet be based on compelling evidence of their effectiveness. The main data that can be brought to bear in favor of such interventions concern the well-established links between the quality of close relationships and health and health-related behaviors (Campbell, 1986; House, Landis, & Umberson, 1988). Second, it can be argued that illness and the promotion of health occur in the context of close relationships and inevitably affect and are affected by these relationships. The question then becomes whether these influences are to be ignored or systematically taken into account. Still, controlled outcome studies are sorely needed.

The focus of this chapter is to examine the specific goals of intervention in close relationships to improve health outcomes. These include working to assist individuals with disabling health problems and their partners to manage the demands of the illness and treatment regimens more effectively; to empower them in their dealings with the health care system; to aid them in the transitions necessitated by illness and disability, including life-style changes; and to help them "put the illness in its place." This latter goal is an important one, particularly in the context of chronic illness, and it deserves more attention than it has received. As described by Gonzalez, Steinglass, and Reiss (1989), it involves striking a balance—striving to meet the demands arising from the illness or disability, but not allowing it to unduly organize or dominate close relationships. Wherever possible, family rituals and traditions are to be maintained, and family members are to be encouraged to continue to pursue goals beyond the management of the health problem.

Family Systems Theory

Family systems theory is an invaluable conceptual framework for understanding illness in close relationships (Ransom, 1989; Weakland, 1977). It calls attention to how individual coping efforts and the outcomes that are achieved are part of and regulated by larger, recurrent patterns of interactions. Close relationships tend to have stabilized patterns of decision making, role allocation, and ways of responding to crises. Change tends to occur within the confines of such a patterning, and the range of options that the individual has depends on the flexibility or adaptability that close relationships afford. The quality of close relationships, how partners react, and how the efforts of partners fit together are all important determinants of what people in close relationships can do in coping with illness. Rather than simply a matter of individual initiative, self-efficacy "thus may reflect the modesty of the demands they face when they have the benefits of a more active and efficacious spouse or one who effectively buffers them from overwhelming stress" (Coyne & Smith, 1994, p. 12). Existing patterns of relationship can be an important resource or an impediment to effective coping with illness and the achievement of positive outcomes, but they rarely can be ignored.

By putting the behavior of people with a disabling illness and their spouses back into its interactional context, family systems theory provides a basis for a nonblaming approach to remedying the problems that arise in their efforts to adjust to the demands of illness. The perspective highlights the paradoxes by which partners may get at cross-purposes to each other and accomplish less than would have been anticipated from their individual resources and commitment to each other (Coyne et al., 1988). For example, following a heart attack, there is a tendency for patients to have higher expectations than their spouses about how much exertion is advisable (Taylor, Bandura, Ewart, Miller, & DeBusk, 1985). A recovering patient getting involved again in the home improvement may alarm his wife by what seems to her to be risky overexertion. She may react by cautioning him, but rather than having its intended effect, this may only prompt him to show her that he can do even more, which further alarms her. The ensuing escalation may be fueled by her sense that he is becoming uncharacteristically stubborn and irrational, and his sense that she is departing from long-standing patterns in their relationship by acting intrusive and bossy. Such relationship issues may then take precedence over any recognition on his part that he is indeed overexerting himself or on hers that yelling at him is not a good strategy for making him see reason. The reciprocal indignation and visible frustration with each other strengthen the new pattern because she fails to appreciate that his "stubbornness" is in reaction to her behavior, and he misses the fact that she is acting out of concern for his welfare.

Chronic and catastrophic illness often confronts intimates with situations in which they have a strong sense of responsibility for the ill person's well-being but a low sense of control. This combination is particularly conducive to such "miscarried helping" in close relationships (Anderson & Coyne, 1990; Coyne et al., 1988). Preexisting problems in communication, illnesses that involve a high degree of uncertainty as to what can be expected or what is the most effective course of action, and a health care system that is ill equipped to facilitate the involvement of family members in health care all contribute to the emergence of such maladaptive patterns of interaction.

Family systems theorists call attention to how the challenges of illness and medical regimens may reorganize interactional patterns. However, there is a sharp division among scholars as to how the role of illness, its symptoms, and its management are to be conceptualized in the context of relationships. More structurally oriented conceptions (Doherty & Baird, 1983; Minuchin, Rosman, & Baker, 1978) involve the notion that difficulties in coping with health problems can become incorporated into relational patterns so that they subsequently prove essential for harmony and regularity. Thus, problems in glycemic control in diabetes come to fit the needs of the relationships in which they occur, perhaps by defusing otherwise intractable conflict over nonhealth issues. Therefore, intervention must focus on restructuring the family so that the health problems are no longer needed. Other family theorists take issue with this idea that health problems serve functions in families (Watzlawick, Weakland, & Fisch, 1974). They caution that glib application of such an idea has led therapists to blame families for problems in managing illness problems that are more appropriately attributed to the vicissitudes of illness or inadequacies in the response of the medical system to the family (Coyne & Anderson, 1988, 1989). From this point of view, families are not presumed to be invested in self-defeating patterns of interaction around health issues. These patterns may persist as a result of misinformation or the belief that what family members are doing is the best or the only thing that can be done under the circumstances. Interventions need only focus on correcting misinformation about the illness or redirecting specific coping efforts, rather than on restructuring family patterns in some fundamental way.

Family systems approaches provide a way of comprehending the dynamic interplay of the illness and how partners cope in the larger context of their lives together. Yet family systems theory is by itself insufficient (Coyne & Fiske, 1992; McDaniel, Hepworth, & Doherty, 1992). It needs to be supplemented by a thorough understanding of specific illnesses, their etiology, manifestations, course and outcomes, and the demands that they place on individuals and their relationships. Professionals cannot always be expected to have an adequate understanding of both family systems theory and the character of particular illnesses, and so they must be prepared to work especially collaboratively with people who have a health problem and their partners and with other professionals. As the following example illustrates, they need to appreciate the limits of interpersonal relationships as explanations for health problems:

> An astute family practice resident noted an association between a middle-aged black woman's trips to the emergency room with uncontrollable asthma attacks and her husband's struggles with racial harassment on the job. The husband was a construction worker, and although a court order had recently forced the integration of largely segregated unions, white workers were making the transition difficult. The resident referred the couple to therapy, where the therapist both impressed and confused them with his observation that the man's management of his wife's medical crises had saved her and distracted him from his overwhelming difficulties at work. The woman was thus rescuing him by providing him with the necessity of rescuing her. For several sessions, the therapist explored this theme while overlooking the recurring pattern of the black man being subject to racial epithets and reacting by compulsively scrubbing himself in long showers and then heavily spraying the house with disinfectant. The woman's trips to the emergency room continued unabated until an attending physician heard about the disinfectant and explained to the man how it precipitated his wife's breathing difficulties. He also gave him a referral for free legal counsel for his job difficulties, but the wife's problems ceased as soon as the man stopped spraying.

Family systems theory is a way of recognizing the relevance of close relationships to health problems and vice versa. Yet if a person is challenged by health problems and is also involved in a close relationship, it does not necessarily follow that health-promoting interventions should focus on this relationship. Indeed, an appreciation of the interpersonal context of problems in coping with illness may lead to the recommendation that the person more effectively take charge of management of an illness and insulate these efforts from the negative influence of close relationships. This may prove a more viable strategy than committing the person's health status to the uncertain outcome of psychotherapy to improve the quality of these relationships. Without adequate assessment of the individual's preferences or the strengths and liabilities of close relationships, the efficacy of enlisting intimates in the management of illness or changing of health-related behaviors may be limited. Moreover, good intentions are not enough: Partners may need guidance as to how to cooperate and to identify what is actually helpful and what is not in what they do. For instance, one study of weight reduction found that either actively involving the husband or instructing him not to get involved produced greater weight loss compared to a control condition.

> The absence of significant differences between the cooperative spouse and the nonparticipating spouse conditions suggests that instructing spouses not to sabotage their wives' efforts may be as effective for long term maintenance as actively training them to aid their wives. (Pearce, LeBow, & Orchard, 1981, p. 236)

Options for Improving Coping

People in close relationships who are experiencing difficulties in dealing with health issues may neither desire nor need conventional marital or family therapy. They may be wary of the implication of a referral that the relationship or partner is being blamed for the health problem. Alternatively, they may view involvement in therapy as an added source of stress when they are already feeling burdened, or they may simply dismiss it as a diversion from the important tasks of managing the illness. The mobilization of support alternatives involving peers (e.g., support groups, self-help groups, dyadic buddies) to supplement deficient or depleted natural networks is another option. When therapy is offered, it is important that objectives be specified clearly (Christie-Seely, 1984; McDaniel et al., 1992). The goal of improving patient outcomes may be facilitated by improvement in the communication or affective involvement of a couple. Yet neither the couple nor the therapist should lose sight of the rationale for having initiated therapy or fail to consider whether there are more direct ways of helping the individual, if that is the goal. Ideally, therapy for medical problems should be brief, problem-oriented, and highly structured (Cade & O'Hanlon, 1993; Fisch, Weakland, & Segal, 1984; Haley, 1973).

Family systems theory is a way of thinking about problems in their interactional context, not a prescription for a particular form of intervention, such as conventional marital or family therapy. More minimalist interpretations of family systems theory encourage involving in therapy only the participants in an interpersonal system who are most distressed with existing patterns and who are willing to consider the possibility of change, not necessarily the whole family or even both partners in a close relationship. The rationale is that the therapist can precipitate change of a more general nature by working with one person to modify his or her specific interactions with others (Coyne, 1987). The Mental Research Institute (MRI) group (Fisch et al., 1984; Watzlawick et al., 1974) has provided case examples of working with spouses to modify behavior of individuals who are unwilling or unable to attend therapy (Hoebel, 1977; Watzlawick & Coyne, 1980). Thus, Watzlawick and Coyne (1980) described working with the wife of a depressed stroke survivor to redirect her well-meant but counterproductive efforts to get him to resume exercise and the normal activities of which he was still capable (see Fisch et al., 1984, for excerpts of a transcript of the therapy sessions). The authors addressed directly the ethical issue involved in such interventions by arguing that successful therapy, even when individually oriented, typically involves an impact on others' behavior. The family systems perspective assumes that people in therapy and those with whom they have close relations are unavoidably influencing each other. The issue is not whether such influence should occur, but how it is to be taken into account in the most humane, ethical, and effective manner.

Therapy is only one of a number of options for intervening in close relationships to improve coping with illness. Another option is the couple-oriented protocol. This is a structured and relatively standardized approach to involving intimates in health care and the change of health-related behaviors. One advantage of such protocols

Table 6.1 Couple Protocol: Post-Myocardial Infarction

I.   Engage spouse
   A.   Explain to patient usefulness of including spouse as a routine practice
   B.   Ask that patient invite spouse to attend a scheduled meeting
   C.   If patient expresses interest but doubts that spouse will come, offer to contact spouse directly
II. Conjoint meeting
   A.   Inquire about recovery process
   B.   Assess style (partnership/collaborative, autonomous, or conflictful) and verify impression by direct inquiry
   C.   Emphasize recovery process is a challenge for both partners
   D.   Inquire about adequacy of information (ask open-ended questions about patient's and spouse's understanding and follow up with queries about specifics)
       1.   Medical aspects of myocardial infarction
       2.   Requested changes in lifestyle
       3.   How active patient can be
       4.   What can be expected for the future
       5.   How much emotional stress patient can handle
       6.   How spouse can be most helpful to patient (invite discussion of this topic in particular)
       7.   Sex after a heart attack
   E.   Inquire about areas of disagreement or conflict and assess necessity of any action
   F.   Inform about Heartbeats Club (peer support) activities for both patients and spouses
   G.   Elicit feedback
III. Possible actions
   A.   None required
   B.   Provide brief advice or suggestions to couple
   C.   Peer counseling through Heartbeats
   D.   Referral for marital or individual counseling

---

is that they take a proactive and preventive approach, encouraging the implementation of effective behavior before problems have developed. They generally involve identifying a specific role for intimates and a set of helpful and unhelpful behaviors with respect to a specific health issue. Alternatively, the couple may be provided with a structured opportunity to discuss the health issue and to negotiate a plan that is more tailored to their particular circumstances. Table 6.1 gives the example of a couples-oriented protocol for use after one partner has had a myocardial infarction.

Couple-oriented protocols would seem to hold considerable promise, yet when they have been subjected to formal evaluation, the results have not been uniformly positive. There have been a few noteworthy demonstrations of the efficacy of spouse involvement in programs for weight loss, smoking cessation, and other lifestyle changes (Brownell, Heckerman, Westlake, Hayes, & Monti, 1978; Morisky et al., 1983), but overall, the literature is best characterized as dominated by mixed and negative results (Brownell & Stunkard, 1981; Lichtenstein, Glasgow, & Abrams, 1986; O'Neil, 1979). Brownell and Stunkard (1981) provided a succinct critique of problems in the interventions that have been evaluated for weight loss and the critique that is more generally applicable:

> The interactions between patients and spouses are complex. Attempts have often been made to alter these interactions and the associated patterns of behavior before these interactions and patterns are clearly understood. Couples training is a potentially powerful approach to treatment, but careful assessment is needed of attitudes, shared eating patterns, and marital coping skills. (p. 1228)

These points are well taken, but more than a decade later, they have not found their mark in outcome studies in which the interventions are based on a better understanding of the interactional context in which they are being attempted.

Groups for individuals with health problems and their families are another form of intervention. They vary greatly in their format and focus. Some are led by health care professionals, but others are run by family members themselves. Health care professionals may have advantages in the accuracy of the health information they provide and the opportunity to strengthen families' ties to the health care system in ways that ensure more effective care. Yet the interests of tertiary medical care settings and families do not always coincide. Some settings encourage a maladaptive passivity on the part of individuals with health problems, and they are indifferent to the needs of family members. Peer-led groups can serve to empower individuals and families to take more assertive roles in health care and assist them in renegotiating their relationships

with the tertiary care system. The ideal group balances collaborative relationships and bidirectional communication with health
care professionals with the need for individual and family autonomy. This serves to avoid both professional dominance and an
unnecessarily adversarial stance on the part of group members.
Unfortunately, this is not possible in all health care settings.

Some groups are seen primarily as sources of emotional support, but others have educational components and include structured efforts to identify common problems and provide mutual
aid in implementing solutions. For instance, some postmyocardial
infarction groups discuss issues such as sexuality that they feel
they cannot talk about with health care professionals, share low-
sodium and low-fat recipes at potluck dinners, and have group
exercise programs. Some diabetes support groups have regular
presentations by health care professionals to keep members informed of new developments in the management of the illness. By
also sharing their own experiences with each other, group members
develop an understanding of the benefits and drawbacks of new
technology that is grounded in actually having to live with it.

There is disagreement concerning whether groups should always include both individuals with health problems and spouses.
Gonzales et al. (1989) argue that groups composed of both can
serve as safe forums for airing differences, and not to include
patients serves only to increase the distance between patients and
spouses. They also cite a finding that involving the partner with
cancer increased family member attendance in an oncology group
(Wellisch, Mosher, & Scoy, 1978). On the other hand, based on
experience with the wives of men with cardiac problems, Anderson
(1983) argues that a group composed only of wives allowed them
to address issues, express themselves, and react in ways that
would not have occurred if their husbands had been present.

In structure and content, psychoeducational groups fall between psychotherapy and more conventional groups and contain
elements of each, but also have their own unique characteristics.
The approach was originally developed in multiple family discussion groups for chronic psychiatric problems (Anderson et al.,
1986), but Gonzales et al. (1989) have described a promising ex-

tension to families coping with physical illness. These groups are composed of people with health problems and their families, and they are brief and highly structured. A case can be made (Gonzales et al., 1989) for including a diversity of illnesses in a single group to highlight the general issues involved in coping with illness, but there are other situations in which more homogeneous groups might be more appropriate.

Gonzales et al. (1989) note that some interventions tend to be focused on either the initial, diagnostic phase of illness or the final phase when the patient is debilitated (groups for caregivers of Alzheimer's patients) or terminally ill. In contrast, these psychoeducational groups are oriented to the long and often indefinite chronic phase. There is a particular concern with the family's revaluation of the appropriateness of coping strategies that were implemented in the acute stress of the initial diagnosis or health crisis, such as a myocardial infarction. Also, most interventions are intended for relationships in which problems in dealing with health issues have already emerged, but these groups are intended to prevent such problems *before* they occur.

The groups involve four to six families coming together for eight weekly sessions, which are divided into three components. In the educational component, families are provided with information, but also encouraged to draw on their own experience to construct a picture of the stresses and strains that are generic to families coping with illness. The individual family issues component builds on the earlier educational phase as each family reviews and reevaluates the particular coping strategies that its members have been employing. The final, affective component focuses on the impact of the illness on the family's emotional life and the various styles for handling emotional issues.

These groups involve a novel, multilevel, shifting, "group-within-a-group" format. At set times, the sessions are variously organized around patients as a group, family members as a group, the individual family as a group, and the broader group of families coping with illness. For instance, in the initial session, patients form a subgroup to discuss and receive validation for their experiences within their families. In the family issues component, the individual families are instructed to come prepared to discuss with one of the group co-leaders the impact of the illness on specific areas of their lives. The other families and the other group leader quietly listen to this discussion, and then the family receives their impressions.

Psychoeducational groups and brief couples and family therapy differ in their format and emphases but share some common assumptions and features. Namely, both are grounded in family systems theory and use it to underscore how illness can render previously effective coping strategies counterproductive, despite the good intentions and intelligence of everyone involved. Thus, they establish a nonjudgmental stance for defining roles and responsibilities in coping with the illness, avoiding blaming of either people with chronic illness or intimates while promoting mutual support and problem solving. Both respect the importance of balancing concern with the demands of management of the illness with the needs of well partners and the requirements for maintaining relationships and having meaningful lives together. Both emphasize proactive efforts to solve concrete practical problems rather than passive learning experiences, but they differ somewhat in how these efforts are promoted.

In problem-focused therapy, there is a greater emphasis on the unique circumstances of a couple and what has been successful for them, but also what is not working, and the resources that are being ignored or misapplied in their existing efforts. Intervention occurs after relationship problems have already developed, and it tends to involve a reworking of patterns of interaction and redirection of coping strategies. Therapy may be organized around identifying and reworking specific patterns of coping or renegotiating specific aspects of the relationship. In psychoeducational groups, structured opportunities are provided for patients and family members to discuss their specific situations and benefit from other families discussing theirs, but there is more emphasis on identifying general themes and normative issues and a less intensive focus on specific families. Although patients and family members may receive a lot of valuable suggestions and feedback, they may not be able to get the sustained guidance needed to change already entrenched patterns.

❧ Influences and Issues in Working With Relationships to Improve Coping With Illness

How people in a close relationship adapt to illness is shaped by a number of influences outside the relationship. In important respects, these relationships can be seen as open, rather than closed, systems, and what transpires in them and what outcomes can be achieved depend on a number of factors other than just the commitment and skills of the people involved. In intervening in these relationships, it is important to consider not only the opportunities for improving outcomes, but also the constraints on what can be accomplished, the limits that are imposed by the illness, and the nature of involvement with the medical system. Overly optimistic expectations about the benefits of improving social support and coping ultimately lead to disappointment, demoralization, and blame. Furthermore, intervention needs to be grounded in an understanding of some key issues and themes, such as gender roles, the developmental tasks being faced by both the relationship and the individuals involved, and the preexisting quality and style of the relationship.

Relationships as Open Systems: Influence of Illness

People do not merely cope *with* their illness, they *are* ill. They and their intimates must contend with the limits it imposes on their functioning, how they can cope, the kinds of relationships that can be had, and the quality of life that is possible. Illnesses differ in the kinds of demands they place on relationships and the degree of difference that changes in support and coping can make. Many illnesses have basic trajectories over which little control can be exercised. Nevertheless, what can be controlled is the extent to which the illness dominates relationships. Some illnesses confront relationships with an asymmetry: Nothing partners do can prevent further deterioration or death, but the failure to adhere to a complicated regimen can hasten it. Thus, with congestive heart failure, a single dietary indiscretion may precipitate a profound medical crisis, but strict adherence to the prescribed diet offers no guarantee that complications and deterioration will be avoided.

Coping efforts are often based on unrealistic expectations about their efficacy. Although this may be adaptive in the early stages of disease, it can lead to guilt and despair when complications develop. Thus, strict control of diabetes may delay neuropathy, but it will not prevent it. Furthermore, there is a great deal of individual variation in the course of diabetes and in the timing of the onset of complications that has nothing to do with adherence. Partners may need guidance in accepting that diseases are unfair in this way and in resisting the tendency to blame themselves for developments that are beyond their control.

It is also important that interventions to assist people not foster unrealistic ideas about the role of stress in the course of disease or the potential for influencing the course of disease by simply reducing stress. Under the influence of the family psychosomatics model (Minuchin et al., 1978), therapists have sometimes oversold the notion that there are direct links between family interaction and physiology. Thus, they have been guilty of focusing on the "reduction of family stress that induces physical symptoms" (Sargent, 1985, p. 205) when it would have been more efficacious to identify and modify treatment adherence to improve physical functioning. Iatrogenic influences are possible. Medical crises create understandable distress and disarray in relationships. However, if the family is then blamed for the complicating events, they may become further demoralized and impaired in their ability to ensure the adherence to regimen that will make another medical crisis less likely.

Relationships as Open Systems:
Influence of the Health Care System

We have found that following a myocardial infarction, the quality of a couple's relationship with the health care system is a crucial determinant of patient self-efficacy and spouse distress (Coyne & Smith, 1991, 1994). The adequacy of the information that is provided to partners while the patient is still hospitalized may set a trajectory for their later adaptation, perhaps because there is so little opportunity for consultation later (Speedling, 1982). Yet particularly in tertiary care settings, efforts to involve and inform family members are inconsistent and sometimes nonexistent. Too little attention is given to whether basic information has been provided to them, whether what has been said has been heard accurately, or how the often abstract and vague admonitions with which they have been provided can be reasonably implemented in their daily routines.

Problems in relation to the health care system are often the source of conflict within close relationships, particularly when couples have contradictory interpretations of the instructions they have been given. Intimates are often left ill informed about prognosis, treatment, and rehabilitation. Aside from being a source of unnecessary anxiety, a lack of information may impair partners' contribution to the individual's well-being and recovery. It would seem that simple interventions by health care personnel could resolve such confusion and conflict. Yet we have found that the normative response of couples to confusing and contradictory advice is to struggle on their own, rather than take the initiative in going back to health care personnel with their concerns (Coyne & Sonnega, 1994). They may need considerable encouragement and support to undertake such efforts.

Writings concerning family therapy and health problems have emphasized the benefits of close collaborative relationships between therapists and health care personnel and of therapists being integrated into health care settings (Doherty & Baird, 1983; McDaniel et al., 1992). Less has been written about the virtues of therapy and health care sometimes being kept separate. Understandable anger and alienation after negative experiences with health care personnel can serve as the impetus to seek psychotherapy. People may need the assurance that therapy is separate from their health care to feel safe in ventilating and then reevaluating their feelings. Furthermore, not all medical personnel appreciate the benefits of family members taking an active, assertive role in health care, and a therapist may need the autonomy of not working in the same setting to avoid the practical and ethical issues entailed in divided loyalties.

Gender in Family Systems

Despite notable efforts to correct it, family systems theorists have operated with considerable gender blindness. Discussions of *families'* coping strategies and *families'* adaptation to illness belie strongly gender-differentiated patterns of interaction, with a disproportionate share of the burden of accommodating illness falling on *women*, whether they are partners or patients themselves (Coyne & Fiske, 1992). As we noted earlier, women are more likely than men to quit work to tend an ill spouse. Men withdraw from household responsibilities and are nurtured by their wives after a myocardial infarction. When women return from the hospital after suffering a myocardial infarction, they are likely to resume light household responsibilities more quickly, attend to family members' needs, and feel guilty about changes in their household responsibilities imposed by their functional limitations. Men do not report such guilt (Hamilton, 1990).

Efforts to improve coping with illness inevitably encounter gender-related issues. Many of the demands imposed by the illness of one spouse are met within the confines of the couple's existing differentiation of roles. Yet catastrophic health events, such as a husband's myocardial infarction, may lead to a negotiation of a more egalitarian marital relationship even when the changes are not necessitated by the husband's impairment (Croog & Levine, 1982). However, there may be cohort effects, so that in couples who are currently late middle-aged and aged, gender-differentiated roles may be so well established that they are relatively immune to the pressures for renegotiation arising from functional impairments of either the husband or the wife.

Health professionals need to be sensitive to how their own assumptions about gender roles affect their work with couples. Do they implicitly defer to the husband's authority or get intimidated by his anger when they intervene in the couple's struggles over who should do what and how? Do they automatically assume that the burden of change will disproportionately fall on women? Men may be less experienced in some household chores than women, but do professionals accept their inefficiency or "ineptitude" as an incapability rather than encouraging men to get the practice they need? Women tend to be socialized into caretaking roles in close relationships (Gilligan, 1982). Although their nurturance may prove to be a crucial resource for couples coping with illness, they may need encouragement to look after themselves as well as an ailing husband. Even if wives understandably lose perspective in the face of a husband's health crisis, professionals should not. Particularly in the transition from an acute event like a myocardial infarction to the long-term regimen and reworking of lifestyle that follows, intervention may need to include a reassertion of the woman's own well-being as a legitimate focus of concern.

Changes in coping strategies entail renegotiation of relationships, and gender differences in strategies and goals may be relevant. Men and women may differ in the importance that they attach to the quality of the marital relationship, their strategies for resolving conflict, and the value they ascribe to ventilating negative feelings as a means of coping with stress (Gilligan, 1982; Gottlieb, in press; Gottman, 1991; Rausch, 1974). Wives are more likely than husbands to base their feelings of well-being on the quality of their marriage and therefore have a greater need to deal with any marital shortcomings (Gottman, 1991). Women also may be more sensitive to expressive dimensions of coping strategies, what is shared or expressed as well as instrumentally accomplished.

It is possible to overemphasize the relevance of gender and thus caricature differences between men and women. Yet this does not take away from the dangers of neglecting these issues and pathologizing reactions that otherwise might be viewed as understandable on the basis of gender differences (Altschuler, 1993). For instance, there has been a distinct misogyny in discussions of "overprotectiveness" as an almost exclusive female failing (Fiske et al., 1991; Walters, Carter, Papp, & Silverstein, 1988). What is missed in such discussions is that high levels of involvement and vigilance may be normative and appropriate to manage the health of a vulnerable patient (Gillis, 1984), and that a certain degree of indulgence may be an effective way of expressing caring and support. Overprotectiveness has been seen as a highly prevalent, motivated, destructive influence on patient recovery. There has been too little consideration of whether heightened involvement in such instances is indeed counterproductive, or, when it is miscarried, whether it reflects anxiety and misinformation rather than hostile intent.

Life Course Issues

Couples' ability to cope with illness and still retain as much of their lives as possible depends on the fit of these tasks with the other developmental tasks they face as couples and as individuals. These other tasks—beginning a family, developing a career, and, later, putting children through college and accumulating the financial resources for retirement—may determine how illness will reverberate throughout their lives. Coping with chronic illness may be a normative task of adult life, but its timing with respect to other tasks varies greatly. Chronic illness and catastrophic health events, such as a myocardial infarction, may prove more devastating for younger couples because of greater interference with pursuit of their other goals (Coyne & Smith, 1991). In contrast, older people may welcome retirement a few years earlier than planned and face a decline in quality of life if they return to work (Radley, 1988).

Older couples have had longer histories within which to develop shared understandings and routines. They may not be any more skilled in resolving conflict, but they may have more practiced ways of avoiding it based on an understanding of each other. When they fit with the tasks of coping with illness, the implicit understandings and shared routines that older couples have accumulated may provide important sources of structure and efficiency. Yet existing patterns may prove difficult to change when they do not fit. There is evidence that older couples benefit less from marital therapy (Schmaling & Jacobson, 1988), perhaps because of a greater rigidity and routine to their patterns of interaction. It may be that interventions to improve their coping with illness need to focus more on accommodating these patterns and fostering mutual understanding and acceptance of the couple's differences rather than attempting to bring about wholesale change in them.

Relationship Quality and Style

There is considerable documentation of the negative impact of marital tension and conflict on health and health-related behaviors, and the apparent benefits of supportive relationships may lie in the absence of such negativity as much as anything else (Coyne & DeLongis, 1986). Hostile criticism may be among the key destructive elements of negative relationships (Coyne, Downey, & Boergers, 1992). It leaves its recipients feeling poorly about themselves and their critics. It impairs problem solving and increases reliance on ineffective ways of dealing with conflict (Baron, 1988). Health crises may sometimes impose a renewed honeymoon period of closeness and cooperation in previously troubled relationships (Speedling, 1982). Each partner may feel a renewed sense of being needed and appreciated by the other, and conflict may be suppressed. Yet with passage of time, the challenges and tasks that brought them closer together may become sources of conflict, and any preexisting tension and dissatisfaction may resurface and intensify. What collaboration there is may take the form of *antagonistic cooperation,* done largely as a matter of obligation and necessity rather than caring, and it may be done with tension and overt hostility rather than appreciation (Coyne & Smith, 1991).

Efforts to cope with illness need to be insulated from the effects of troubled relationships, particularly hostile criticism, and intervention should not presuppose more cooperation than can be reasonably expected. Yet beyond such simple statements, there is little empirical basis for posing indications or counterindications for intervention or suggesting how intervention should be tailored to the existing style or patterning of a relationship. We may assume that different relationships call for different strategies and goals, but the research literature does not provide much guidance.

Even if lacking an empirical basis, a simple typology proposed by Jaffe and Jordan-Marsh (1983) seems to have heuristic value. They distinguish among three broad styles of relationships. A *collaborative* or *partnership* style is characterized by mutuality, shared decision making, and a mix of shared and independent activities. Efforts to cope with illness and health regimens are likely to be characterized by a division of labor and a preservation of other activities and commitments. Presumably, intervention should be able to draw a sense of cooperation but still respect the independent pursuits of the patient and partner. In contrast, members of an *autonomous* couple make independent decisions, share relatively few activities, and have learned to tolerate their differences. Efforts to cope with illness and health regimens are likely to be kept separate from other aspects of the relationship. Intervention might accommodate this set of preferences, except where the impairment of the patient or demands of health regimens require a reorientation. Partners in *enmeshed* couples make unilateral decisions that are met with opposition, misunderstanding, and blaming. They share most activities, do relatively few things independently, but lack a sense of collaboration or mutual enjoyment. Efforts to cope with health issues are likely to be characterized by conflict and power struggles. Intervention might focus on taking the health regimen out of the struggle, perhaps by allocating roles and responsibilities in a well-specified and unambiguous manner so that efforts at negotiation and collaboration that would prove conflictful are not routinely necessary.

This typology clearly implies that one type of couple, the enmeshed, is likely to have greater difficulty coping with illness. Yet this typology also suggests that other couples do best if there is a fit between the way in which changes are implemented and the existing style of the couple. As with any typology, however, it is important to keep in mind its limitations. Are these patterns always so pervasive? Even when couples generally may be characterized as partnership, autonomous, or enmeshed, there may be key departures from this style, areas of their lives in which the decisions and activities of the couple are quite different. Therapists need to be alert to the emergence of such exceptions and help the couple to build on them when they are in the service of improving their coping with illness.

❧ Some Interventions

Providing Information

People with disabling health problems and their partners may have more regular contact with the professionals involved in providing psychosocial intervention, whether it takes the form of a psychoeducational/support group or formal therapy, than they do with physicians or other professionals more directly involved in their health care. Consequently, problems in managing the illness, misinformation, or the emergence of complications or side effects might be disclosed first in group or therapy. It becomes important for professionals to have a clear sense of the limits of their role, and although they may assist the people with health problems and their partners in interpreting their experiences, they should avoid practicing medicine. They still may have a valuable role to play in assisting couples in engaging the medical system and articulating their concerns in a way that gets appropriate attention. Groups and therapy can have an important function in helping participants make sense of the bewildering complexity, impersonality, and even indifference of the medical system so that they do not blame themselves for its shortcomings or fail to get the care they deserve.

Groups and therapy also provide information about predictable difficulties in managing illness and some of the relevant interpersonal processes. It is helpful when patients and intimates can appreciate that much of their struggle may be normative or expected under the circumstances and not a reflection of personal defect or incompatibility. Information is best provided in a context of bidirectional communication, with the expertise of the professional balanced by the greater familiarity of the couple with their own circumstances and experience. It is not assumed that they necessarily lack knowledge about how to get along. Rather, they may nevertheless get caught up in patterns that do not reflect what they know. Thus, most people report that they do not find advice from intimates an effective form of support, but they resort to it when trying to help their partners (Lehman, Ellard, & Wortman, 1986). Similarly, most people appreciate that the constructiveness of criticism is only in the intention of the person who delivers it, not the impact on the recipient, yet we all find ourselves slipping into it without thinking. This indicates that peers and professionals are valued for informational appraisal support and partners for emotional support (Dakof & Taylor, 1990).

Reframing

Reframing refers to a therapeutic strategy involving acknowledging a person's existing view of a situation but calling attention to an alternative focus or interpretation in a way that allows different emotional reactions and coping strategies to emerge (Coyne, 1985; Watzlawick et al., 1974). Very often it entails giving a positive connotation or more charitable reinterpretation to another's behavior so that a more sympathetic response is forthcoming. Thus, a man's stubborn resistance to influence, and, notably, to his wife's suggestion that he take better care of himself, might be reframed as the last refuge of his pride and self-respect after his stroke had taken so much away from him. The intention is that she not take his response so personally or respond so harshly when she is unable to influence him. Reframing may also assist a person in reflecting on and disavowing an unhelpful way of responding: "I know you mean well, but your harassing your wife about her diet lets her off the hook. She no longer has to struggle with how hard it is to stick to it. She can simply decide not to be pushed around by you and rebel against you, not the diet, with that justification."

Reframes often involve providing succinct metaphors that serve to reorganize coping efforts. Thus, a woman who may be having difficulty allowing herself any time for activities that are not directly related to caring for her husband might be given the metaphor of the oxygen mask on an airliner: "In the event of a decompression, please adjust your own mask before trying to be of assistance to anyone else. That way, you will be much more effective." Subsequently, the woman can remind herself with the metaphor and expect a follow-up question each session concerning what, aside from taking care of her husband, she has done to adjust her own oxygen mask.

Gonzales et al. (1989) discuss the value of using metaphors to externalize the illness so that partners can blame it without blaming the person with the health problem. Externalizing the problem ("Sometimes diabetes gets between you and your partner. . . . Have you two managed to hold your own against the diabetes this week?") is intended to decrease unproductive conflict and encourage the couple to join together against the illness (White & Epston, 1990). Thus, in one case, an illness was described as a " 'two-year old-terrorist' who rules the family with excessive and unpredictable demands and threatens catastrophic consequences if the demands are not met" (Gonzales et al., 1989, p. 78). In a similar vein, the spouse of a person with diabetes might be advised to consider her harshness and cursing when she wakes up in a hypoglycemic state to be her diabetes speaking.

Reorganizing Patterns of Coping

Efforts to reorganize coping efforts sometimes take the form of a process of explicit negotiating. Thus, partners might identify what is helpful and unhelpful in each other's behavior and offer to make changes, either in quid pro quo fashion or by simply having discovered that some strategies do not work as intended. Sometimes, it is a matter of jarring the existing pattern so that the couple discovers a more productive way of coping. A man who had just days or weeks to live and his wife had gotten locked into an unfortunate struggle in their discussion of what she was going to do after his death. At the point of consultation, the pattern would be repeated regularly with the woman crying and seeking his comfort, saying, "I don't know how I am going to make it. I am going to miss you so much," to which he would reply with annoyance, "No, you are not. You are all set." This would upset her further, and she would protest that he did not appreciate how much he meant, and he would reply with something like, "Rubbish, you're all set," and get angry, cutting off the discussion. The therapist spoke to each of them separately and gave each an opportunity to express his or her frustration with the pattern in which they were stuck. He then met with them together at the man's bedside. He started by telling them that they were more than a match for him.

> I am afraid I am not very helpful. You two are more than a match for me. [To the husband:] She's stubbornly trying to tell you that it

does not matter how well off she is going to be financially, there is no one like you in the world. You're busy trying to get reassurance that she knows she should not worry because you have provided for her so well. [To the wife:] You are trying to express your caring the only way you know how, by letting him know how worried you are about needing him and missing him. You're hurt by your inability to get across to him how special he is. You feel dismissed and rejected. [To the husband:] You're hurt and defeated by her still worrying after you tried so hard to protect her from having to worry. You feel your efforts have been rejected. I'm stuck and we are not being given much time. Who is the most stubborn of the two of you?

Each nominated the other, and then the three of them sat in silence until the man reached out to his wife. The therapist then asked if each could speak his or her piece without interruption, starting with her. This time they did it warmly, comforting each other.

Patterns are often renegotiated with such "shuttle diplomacy": the therapist initially meeting with each partner separately. However, sometimes a therapist may have to work with one partner to instigate the process when the other initially refuses to participate. Thus, one woman sought therapy by herself without telling her husband. The couple had been characterized by bitter feuding and mutual accusations around the issue of the man's not accepting his need to stop smoking and diet after a myocardial infarction. The woman was encouraged to go home with the following message:

> I went to see a therapist because I have been worried sick about you, and I don't know what to do. I'm not perfect, and I do not always do the right thing, but I am so worried about losing you.
>
> All the therapist would say was that I could not change you. What I can do is say that I worry and admit I cannot change you, but that isn't much help. I guess, though, it is up to you. I can only tell you how I feel and how I care about what happens to you and leave it up to you.

The intended outcome of such an intervention is that when not faced with her anger, the man would be more responsive to her distress and concern about him. To the extent that she has any influence at all, it is a matter of relying on the strength of their relationship, not her cajoling and accusations. Her helplessness and distress need to become problems for them to solve together. The therapist in this example focused on *her* behavior, not because she was at fault but because she was open to trying something different.

Couples often are able to find the resources to renegotiate their relationship on their own when one partner is able to enlist the other with an expression of caring and a sincere acknowledgment of a lack of control over the other's behavior. This is particularly likely when reciprocating anger has been the usual pattern. In other instances, a partner's abandoning of coercive strategies does not immediately improve the patient's health-related behaviors, but sets the stage for cooperation later, when there is increased willingness to admit need. Furthermore, when individuals are deficient in their concern for their own health, they will nevertheless sometimes take positive steps because not to do so would upset someone about whom they care.

Conclusion: Promises, Promises?

More than 15 years after John Weakland's (1977) seminal article "Family Somatics: A Neglected Edge," interventions in close relationships remain a neglected edge in efforts to improve coping with illness. This chapter is meant to convey an enthusiasm for the range and potential of such interventions, but at the same time, recognize that there is lack of outcome data demonstrating that such interventions are effective. Furthermore, there is good reason to believe that they can be ineffective and, at times, even negative in their outcome. Working with close relationships to improve health outcomes and to improve the quality of life when there is illness requires knowledge and skills that many marital and family therapists do not have. It requires a sensitivity to the character of illness and to the reciprocating influences of illness on relationships and relationships on illness. It also requires sensitivity to the degree to which a couple or family's ability to cope with illness is dependent on a health care system that is not always prepared to involve them in any systematic way. Such work also requires humility: Coping and social support are not the only factors affecting health and social outcomes, and they may not be the decisive ones.

Interventions in close relationships to improve coping with illness need to be systematized to the point that controlled outcome studies are possible. Provocative case examples are not enough. Intervention is not yet justified by data. Yet just as unjustified is the more usual pattern of excluding spouses and family members from routine involvement in health care and then automatically assuming that they will meet the demands of coping with illness without assistance. We need to develop a database for decisions regarding when and how to involve family members, but until such data are available, families must be acknowledged to have a legitimate and vital role in health care.

7

Close Relationships,
Chronic Illness,
and Research

All of the study of relationships needs to be placed more strongly within the social contexts that surround dyadic relating (Allan, 1993; Duck, 1993a, 1993b). We have been remiss and lethargic in our efforts to understand how external influences channel relational behaviors (Baxter, 1993; Klein & Milardo, 1993; Wood, 1993)—for example, how the reactions of others to one's personal circumstances affect relationships, as when we become ill or unemployed, or are caught having an affair, or fall in love and wonder whether to tell other people about it (Baxter & Widenmann, 1993). Such tasks are far more complex than the challenges we have hitherto set ourselves as a field and will take much time and energy to accomplish, but are also exciting ones for us to wrestle with if we really want to understand functioning relationships.

(Duck, 1994, p. 159)

Over the past two decades, relationship research has evolved beyond simplistic dyadic conceptualizations to uncover the complex tapestry of relationships, woven of individuals tightly and loosely connected in an amazing variety of ways. This tapestry of relationships is forever being shaped by contexts that include jobs, family, social change, and significant life events, such as career advancement, unemployment, marriage, childbirth, divorce, and health problems. The defining features of a relationship, and the selection of those relationships that are deemed to be "close," will be based, in great measure, on the relationship processes that evolve from these contexts.

In this book, we have focused our attention on the qualitative and quantitative research examining interpersonal relationships within the context of illness and disability. In examining the issue of illness, however, we wish to expand our understanding not only of relationships and health problems, but of human relationships in general. The study of disabling health problems is not a topic to be reserved for those with an interest in illness. It has theoretical import for the overall conceptualization of relationships that guide research, service, and policy. Throughout the book, we have been discussing many basic relational processes: social support, social exchange, relationship maintenance and change, interdependence, life events/stressors and relationships, and relationship-focused coping. How these processes are played out in illness provides a window for observing relationships in chronic stress situations.

Each of the three themes of the relationship process framework presented in Chapter 1, *relationship change, relational supports and stressors*, and *relationship-focused coping*, represent interrelated dimensions that will need to be considered in the study of relationship functioning in illness as well as in other domains of significant life change. In the remainder of the chapter, we highlight concepts and questions specific to relationships and illness that will require more theoretical and empirical attention in future research efforts. These conceptual issues are presented within the three relationship process themes that have formed the framework of the book, followed by some perspectives on methodology.

❧ Relationship Change

There is increasing evidence that illness and disability change social networks and relationships. Illness intrudes on the roles and pleasures that originally constituted close relationships with family and friends. Changes include reduced social network size; increased marital and family difficulties; reduced frequency and spontaneity in social contacts; the termination of activity-based (work, leisure, and community) contacts; and difficulties in companionate activity, support, and communication. There is also considerable loneliness and social isolation among people with disabilities and their significant others. A primary goal for researchers, practitioners, and policymakers is the ability to identify which factors support and which factors constrain relationship quality and personal well-being for people with disabling health problems and their close relationships. We discuss a number of illness and relationship factors and suggest several relationship topics that merit further research.

The Need for Theoretical Integration

Research in this area has proceeded in the absence of a unified theoretical framework. Variants of a general stress and coping paradigm have been applied to understand the stress-distress relations that are observed in the context of illness and disability. As noted earlier, these models have been overly individualistic in focus and have failed to account for the dynamic interpersonal processes that are relevant not only to the outcome of coping *with* disability but to the goals of coping *in* disability.

Theoretical models that have been used in relationship research may be usefully applied to the study of relationships and disability. For example, interdependence theory has been the guiding framework for the bulk of research on commitment, relationship satisfaction, and relationship maintenance (Kelley & Thibaut, 1978; Rusbult & Buunk, 1993). A basic tenet of interdependence theory is that individuals in relationships strive to maintain a dynamic equilibrium of the costs and rewards of activities. If a relationship was in a cost-reward equilibrium prior to the onset of disability, then it is likely that disability will disrupt this equilibrium. Disability becomes a forum for observing the forces that are mobilized to address the issue of equilibrium. In the case of chronic illness, an equilibrium similar to preillness onset might not be reinstated.

It is generally assumed that people who are in relationships have a degree of commitment to their relationship and are motivated to enact behaviors designed to keep the relationship together. Partners may have as their goal the continued existence of the relationship or may aspire to the higher goal of maintaining a certain degree of quality in their relationship (Dindia & Canary, 1993). The goals themselves and the manner in which they are sought may change as a function of disability.

However, beyond the balance sheet of rewards and costs, commitment to relationship maintenance may be influenced by personal values about relationship responsibilities that may make relationships more robust to inequities in relationship resources. The differential impact of commitment beliefs and social exchange on relationship maintenance may change as a function of disability. It is interesting to speculate that in relationships where one partner has a disability, social norms concerning caretaking responsibilities may be a primary determinant of relationship maintenance, whereas these norms may be less significant in relationships where there is not a partner with a disability.

Although we have touched on many aspects of relationship functioning in this book, several important topics have been virtually ignored. These topics include sexuality, dating, acquaintance formation, relationship termination hostility and abuse, and support groups; how people in relationships deal with practical issues such as institutionalization, finance, preparation for death, or euthanasia; and the functioning of specific types of relationships such as relationships with parents, siblings, children, or work relationships. Again, these areas will have to be addressed within the context of a guiding theoretical framework.

Illness, Relationships, and Life Stage

Much of the work discussed in this book has been on acquired disabilities resulting from neurological or vascular events. One characteristic of these disabilities is that they typically occur in middle or later adulthood, in the context of well-established relationships. But other disabilities, such as head injuries and spinal injuries, are more likely to occur in early adulthood and may have a more significant impact on relationship development than on relationship maintenance. The dating settings of contemporary society, including dance halls, bars, movie theaters, and restaurants, may not be readily physically or socially accessible to young individuals with disabilities. As noted earlier, statistics indicate that people with disabilities are more likely to be single than people without disabilities. For people with disabilities, the task of establishing a romantic relationship may present a host of seemingly overwhelming challenges. Beyond anecdotal reports, little attention has been given to the role of life stage in disability and relationship development.

Illness Communication in Relationships

The work of Flor and Turk points to the significant role of the nondisabled spouse in determining the degrees of illness behavior displayed by the spouse with the disability. An important component of this work is that illness behavior may evolve to serve a substantial communicative function in the relationship. The interpersonal control afforded by symptom presentation has been the focus of considerable discussion in some areas of study (Mechanic, 1972) but has yet to be addressed in the context of relationship research.

Illness and Disability as Opportunities
for Relationship Development

As discussed earlier, illness sometimes improves existing relationships, and it is also a venue for the establishment of new relationships. For example, treatment and rehabilitation provide important contexts for relationship development for people with chronic illness and disability. Being thrown into a new social environment containing health professionals, patients, peers in similar health circumstances, and support groups may place constraints on the maintenance of existing relationships, but may also create opportunities for the development of new relationships (Borkman, 1990; Mathews, 1983). Common knowledge and shared experience are important features of relationships (Planalp & Garvin-Doxas, 1994), and the common knowledge of the illness experience provides a rather special kind of bond between those who have disabilities and between patients and therapists. Marriages between health professionals and patients are not uncommon and may suggest the relationship-making potential of hospitals and other treatment settings. Researchers have yet to devote energy to examining positive outcomes.

ะ Relationship Supports and Stressors in Coping

Relationships contribute both *supports* and *stressors* in coping with illness and disability. Although most friends and family members are probably well intentioned, efforts at social support provision may misfire because the perceived support needs of parties differ, because of overinvolvement, or because of underinvolvement. Support provision may result in major distress for primary caregivers, and their needs for emotional and practical support must be addressed.

If caregivers are not overburdened, caregiving can contain a very special set of rewards, such as caring for a loved one and/or seeing the caregiver role as an "occupation" where one develops a high level of skill and expertise in understanding an illness and dealing with its symptoms (Mingo, 1993; Toseland, Rossiter, & Labrecque, 1989).

In the research literature, there have been both agreements and conflicts with respect to the contribution of relationships to adaptation. There is considerable confusion about coping and adaptation, including their conceptualization and measurement, the impact of coping strategies on well-being, and what should constitute markers of adjustment or adaptation.

Social Support as More Than Help

Although much of the relationship research with respect to illness has focused on direct aid received from significant others, we assert that the relational and support needs of people with health problems also include attachment, social validation, intimacy, companionship, pleasure in shared activity, cooperation, and reciprocity. Conceptualizing support purely as provision of aid may exclude other important processes and functions of relationships such as social exchange and equity, the maintenance of social structure, and communal problem solving, all affecting the individual's well-being and ability to cope with illness stressors.

Individual and Relational Differences in Adaptive Success

Certain personality styles, particularly those that are defined in relation to an interpersonal orientation (e.g., dependency, dominance, extroversion) may have a significant influence on the relational challenges that accompany disability. For example, for individuals who possess a highly independent interpersonal style, considerable stress may be experienced with being the recipient of care. Discomfort with receiving care may be expressed as hostility or rejection, placing added strain on the relationship. By contrast, individuals who possess a more dependent interpersonal style may experience comfort as opposed to stress as the recipient of care.

Similar considerations may determine the degree to which individuals experience caregiver stress. Individuals who view caregiving as consistent with their interpersonal or social orientation may adapt to the demands of caregiving with greater ease than will those who view caregiving to be incongruent with their interpersonal or social orientation.

Illness Stressors and Personal Growth

In identifying the stressors of illness, one can overemphasize the frailty of people with a disability. Unfortunately, not enough attention has been paid to how such challenges also contribute to personal growth. People with disabilities seem to have remarkable abilities to make major adaptations in their lives. Does this experience with illness strengthen one's ability to deal with difficult life circumstances? Such an idea was expressed in the following accounts from a Canadian report on disability:

> It is a myth that disabled people are emotionally fragile and therefore, they must be protected from the harsh realities of life. Disabled people are constantly adjusting on a daily basis to difficulties that many people face only in a crisis. So who are the sheltered people in our society? (J. Green, rheumatoid arthritis) (Government of Canada, 1981, p. 10)

> People say to me: "I never could of adjusted the way you have done." And I always tell them: "Of course you could."
> That's what being human is all about, this ability that we have to adjust to new circumstances, no matter how limiting. Regardless of how difficult things get, and I don't minimize that, we have a flexibility of thought and emotion which enables us to make the best of our situation. I'm not unusual in this. I see people making greater adjustments all the time. (I. Parker, quadriplegic due to a diving accident) (Government of Canada, 1981, p. 88)

Linkages Between Individual Coping and Relationships

Obviously, there are linkages among the nature of individual coping profiles and the nature of personal relationships and support processes. Dunkel-Schetter et al. (1987) have argued that coping strategies used by one partner provide cues to significant others about support needs. However, as we discussed in Chapter 4, Davis-Ali et al. (1994), in studying couples in which one partner had had a kidney transplant, have found that the nature of coping strategies is influenced by relationship quality and social support provision. Patients who reported receiving more support from their significant other used more cognitive restructuring and fewer avoidant strategies (such as problem avoidance and social withdrawal) than did those with less perceived support. Interestingly, the authors also found that individual coping was not significantly related to the amount of stress experienced by the significant other, and that the amount of support given by the significant other was not related to the coping strategies used by the patient (Mechanic, 1972). More research needs to be conducted on this topic to clarify the connection between relationship quality, support processes, and coping.

Relationships and Illness Course

An important question that emerges from the area of relationships and disability is whether relationships influence illness course or the severity of disability. The work of Kiecolt-Glaser et al. (1985) suggests that supportive relationships may have an impact on enumerative and functional indexes of immune functioning. The implication is that the presence or absence of supportive relationships may alter immune function in a manner that may place individuals at lower or higher risk for illness onset or illness progression.

The mechanism by which relationships may influence illness course remains largely unknown. One possibility is that the phenomenological experience of support may give rise to processes that affect the pathophysiology of illness activity. Alternately, supportive relationships may influence illness course by facilitating health behaviors such as compliance to medication or dietary regimes (Burman & Margolin, 1992).

❧ Relationship-Focused Coping

People with health problems and their significant others make substantial relationship modifications because of illness. These modifications may be made because of concern for the welfare of others, and so coping strategies may be aimed at significant others rather than at their own distress. In addition, some of the emotional and instrumental stressors of an illness may be handled communally (shared) rather than addressed individually. Coping efforts also may be directed toward restructuring social networks and relationships to better accommodate illness and disability. This may mean appraisals involving revaluing the self in relationships and/or redefining the elements that formerly constituted one's definition of relationship quality. Relationship-focused coping may involve termination of less valued relationships to preserve social energy for the people who matter most. Many issues of relationship-focused coping deserve attention. How do people actually deal with the challenges of illness and disability in their relationships? How can the quality of relationships be maintained or improved through illness and disability? Is there a set of "homestyle adaptational remedies" that people commonly use that are effective in relationship maintenance?

Does Relationship-Focused Coping Need to Be Reciprocal?

Is the retention of a relationship predicated on mutual decision making and action, or can it be maintained by an imbalance in persistence by one of the members? Efforts given to relationship adaptation may have something to do with the prioritization of individual versus relational agendas (e.g., the advancement of one's career as compared with the well-being of individuals who do not possess a strong individual agenda). Each one of us has an individual agenda in relationships and some options to leave a relationship if this agenda becomes unfeasible. Perhaps that is why younger marriages often end in divorce when a member becomes disabled. In such circumstances, few items on the list of relational wants have yet been addressed. I want a family. I want a reasonable income. I want us to engage in lots of activities, trips. I'm just getting started in my career. I don't wish to give it all up to be caregiver.

Social Schemas

Social cognition, especially the concept of schema formation (Taylor & Crocker, 1981) in social relationships may be helpful in examining the ability to restructure relationships and networks following disability. In response to the human need for predictability, understanding, and control, we may develop cognitive schemas of individuals in our social networks that contain information about their identity, behavior, attitudes, and the nature of our relationship with them. The onset of serious health problems, with their accompanying identity and lifestyle changes, requires the reformatting of this cognitive map. The desire and ability to undertake this process, as well as the nature of the reformatted map, may explain why relationships of disabled people change. This process may require continuing attention to address changes of people with degenerative health problems so that people who have a strong need for predictability or who lack flexibility may opt out of these relationships.

The Intended Beneficiary of Coping Efforts

I may survive this ordeal, but will my relationship? Where shall I place my coping resources: for the benefit of my own well-being or significant others, or the well-being of relationships? In the examination of coping, a major issue is sorting out the intended beneficiary of coping efforts: the individual with the condition, significant other(s), and/or the relationship. Efforts intended for one party may result in loss for another. For instance, actions that benefit the individual or significant others may not necessarily benefit the relationship. A newly married individual diagnosed with a degenerative illness may push for a divorce to free up a mate to establish an "illness-free" marital relationship unburdened by the perceived constraints imposed by illness. This coping strategy is contrived to benefit the mate, but obviously not intended to benefit the maintenance of the marriage (Gottlieb & Wagner, 1991).

Relationship Dialectics

In Chapter 5, we simplified relationship-focused coping for the purpose of presentational clarity; however, in reality, coping attempts will be related to the coping goals and strategies of significant others. Therefore, the process and direction of relationship-focused coping will vary across dyads and over time. These factors will create dynamic relational tensions, which have been discussed as dialectics. The study of relationship dialectics is fairly new and has focused on tensions that seem to be generic to relationships (Baxter, 1990, 1994; Montgomery, 1993). It may be useful to build on this base by applying relationship dialectical tensions to the design of relationship-focused coping strategies. Several illness-relationship dialectical themes have been developed (Lyons & Meade, 1995). For instance, the *personal control dialectic* is the tension between independence and reliance. Maintenance of identity and self-worth are tied to the perceived ability to control the illness, minimize its intrusiveness, and be independent. An example of the personal control dialectic is given in the following account from a women with MS.

> If you don't have someone you can ask to do things, then I think what happens is . . . you're swamped. Because you're trying to keep a positive outlook for the family, for the people that you know. And if you've got frustration building up inside you because you can't do things, then that frustration vents itself on the people that you don't want to be on the other end of it. You want them to see you as someone who can deal with things. (Lyons & Meade, 1995, p. 204)

Another dialectic is the *attachment dialectic,* the tension between withdrawal and enmeshment in the face of disability. At the withdrawal end of the dialectic, illness is addressed through a reduction in closeness and intimacy. At the other end of the dialectic is *enmeshment*, Minuchin's (1974) term for overly attached individuals whose identities are tightly connected to the relational unit. At the enmeshment end of the dialectic, individuals become more tightly connected, resulting in overprotectiveness, helplessness, and a lack of individual freedom. A midpoint emerges as an *interdependence orientation* (Coyne et al., 1991). This perspective emphasizes the needs and goals of both relational partners and the coordination of these needs and goals. Rather than the illness preventing participation in shared activities, previously shared activities are adapted or new activities are initiated to ensure sustained involvement. Research needs to examine whether a dialectical approach is useful in understanding coping with illness, and how dialectical tensions influence the nature and extent of relationship-focused coping.

Interventions

How can interventions influence the process of coping and adaptation in relationships? Coyne (Chapter 6) used family systems theory to conceptualize coping in a relationship context and presented strategies for improving coping in this context. Several forms of couple, family, and peer group interventions were examined. A problem-focused approach was recommended, with emphasis on issue clarification and the identification of coping resources, and taking into consideration gender issues and the recognition of a couple's relational quality and style. Nevertheless, it may be very difficult to change entrenched patterns of behavior. Studies that examine the processes and outcomes of such intervention are necessary in establishing the role of health care services in facilitating relationships' coping with disabling health problems.

Characteristics of Relationships, Networks, and Societies

Why do certain relationships adapt to illness more readily than others? Is there something that one might term a hardy or resilient relationship, a relationship that can withstand external threats such as illness? One might speculate on a few of the hardy relationship's characteristics: obviously, a strong sense of commitment to relationship maintenance; a history of coping with stressors that has increased competence; kin and societal values and supports to maintain the relationship; a communal coping orientation in which illness stressors are shared; a relationship that is flexible, not easily threatened by change or ambiguity; and instrumental coping resources, such as finances.

If one could prepare a network for illness, what would that network be like? Some characteristics worthy of investigation include density, proximity, inclusion of a member who is particularly competent around illness issues and who can mobilize others, and a network that perceives illness as a communal issue and is committed to the well-being of its members. Milardo and Wellman (1992) state that every relationship between two people is conditioned by their separate and mutual relationships with others, and this was highlighted in the Gary and Eleanor scenario in Chapter 1. Close relationships do not exist in isolation, but function in networks, particularly in the presence of illness. For instance, the maintenance of friendships through illness in older adults is influenced by family relationships (Johnson, 1983). Friendship maintenance for the person with a disability may be facilitated by family members who encourage interaction. Having a group of buddies visit a friend with cancer may reduce the fear each individual has of making the first contact. Kurt Vonnegut (1989) comments about the importance of viewing marriage in a wider relationship context:

> Of necessity we are such solitary nomads, no matter what our race or class, that few of us are governed by the customs and attitudes of a stable extended family in the immediate neighborhood. . . . Marriage for human beings without extended families is a two-character play without a backstage crew and far worse, without an audience out front that gives a damn. This is tough, even if nobody gets sick. (p. 71)

Relationships are patterned by the social, economic, cultural, and biographical contexts in which they exist (Allan, 1993). The cultural norms and rules around relational responses to illness are an important component for understanding both support and relationship processes. However, multicultural perspectives are yet a small portion of research on the topics of relationships, social support, coping, and disability.

Societal change also affects the relationship-illness experience. Network structures and functions themselves have become increasingly diverse and transient (e.g., later marriages, decisions not to marry, marital instability, single-parent families, gay and lesbian relationships, and dual career couples). As indicated throughout the book, gender is a central feature in coping and adaptation. Although women traditionally have been responsible for health, illness, and relationship maintenance, are responsibilities shifting with the changing social roles of women?

What kind of relational life do we wish to make available to a person with health problems? What sort of financial and human investment are we prepared to make, realizing the potential of it happening to us all? Societal changes that would increase the quality of relationships for people with a disability include greater physical and social accessibility of community life, increased value placed on disabled individuals, careful consideration of such changes as residential moves that may affect proximity to friends and family, and increased relational competence by both disabled people and their significant others.

A key issue is change to the health care system that must provide for comprehensive models of service delivery for people with chronic health problems and disabilities. Most health care systems currently operate from an acute care model. Another important need is the availability of funds for psychosocial research on chronic illness and disability. Many health agencies that are concerned with chronic illness must make funds available for research other than biomedical science so that appropriate rehabilitation and community services are developed to increase quality of life. Unfortunately, the topics of prevention and cure are more appealing than the topic of living well with a chronic health problem.

Society's representations of illness and disability may not be efficacious for individuals with a disability and for their relationships. How can societal attitudes, services, and policies facilitate relationship and support processes? How do we address the gender roles in this as well as public versus family roles? Should norms/rules around relationships and health problems be clarified and strengthened? How do we teach people to be more comfortable and relationally competent around disability? Is there something like "relational efficacy and disability," and, if so, how might we identify its features? In addressing all of these questions, there is obvious value in conducting cross-cultural, anthropological, and ethics research.

Methodological Issues

Issues of physical accessibility of buildings, transportation, and consideration of disabilities such as cognition, hearing, vision, fine and gross motor skills, and energy can be major challenges in the design of research methods that can reach, be understood by, and be relevant to people with disabilities. General relationship surveys may miss important features of relationship functioning salient to the presence of disability. Obviously, issues of social validation, social exchange, intimacy, loneliness, and social support are going be important relationship dimensions.

It is our position that both qualitative and quantitative methodologies are required to examine fully the complexities of close relationships through illness and disability. Together, they contribute to our understanding of the social experience of illness, including such topics as coping, social support provision, relationship functioning, and relationship quality.

Hendrick (1986) has noted:

> If behavioral analyses provide a solid external structure for research in intimate relationships, then perhaps descriptive, phenomenological approaches can craft the richly colored and textured furnishings that will complete the building process of the study of human relationships. (p. 336)

This statement suggests that a major purpose of qualitative research is to provide details for a framework already established by empirical research. In addition to this benefit, systematic qualitative research can provide a valuable means of generating theory, research questions, and insights into instrument development. Qualitative procedures may be particularly useful for the study of relationship processes in understudied populations, such as people with disabling health problems.

Very few studies actually have compared relationship effects within social networks or across illnesses. An obvious gap relates to nondisabled companions' perceptions of disability in close relationships. There is a need for comparative research on relationship adaptation, change, and quality from the perspectives of the individual with the condition *and* significant others.

Most work has been cross-sectional versus longitudinal. Few studies have examined coping or relationship processes through the experience of illness, although notable exceptions include the work of Davis-Ali et al. (1994), Gottlieb et al. (1991), and Sullivan, Mikail, et al. (1992). The ideas on relationship-focused coping presented in Chapter 5 arise from exploratory qualitative research with small numbers of respondents and therefore are very speculative at this point. These data give some insight into "perceived" relationship processes but offer little insight into relationship preservation or enhancement (Theme 1), or relational supports and stressors (Theme 2). These are exciting and important areas for further research.

ẽ Conclusion

Most participants in relationships will experience health problems and disabilities that challenge the maintenance of these relationships and create the need for relationship-focused coping efforts. Although society has promoted an ideology of social integration, relationship problems and challenges persist. Most interventions on integration have focused on social policy and legal issues, but little attention has been paid to addressing interpersonal difficulties, particularly in established relationships. With the demands of everyday life, there must be serious consideration to addressing relationship issues such as relationship adaptation and maintenance, commitment, social exchange, and social norms related to chronic illness and disability. This consideration will, in the final analysis, determine the fate of such relationships.

References

Adams, J. E., & Lindemann, E. (1974). Coping with long-term disability. In J. E. Adams (Ed.), *Coping and adaptation* (pp. 127-139). New York: Basic Books.

Adams, R. G. (1985). Emotional closeness and physical distance between friends: Implications for elderly women living in age segregated and age integrated settings. *International Journal of Aging and Human Development, 22,* 55-75.

Adams, R. G., & Blieszner, R. (1994). An integrative conceptual framework for friendship research. *Journal of Social and Personal Relationships, 11,* 163-184.

Ahern, D. K., Adams, A. E., & Follick, M. J. (1985). Emotional and marital disturbance in spouses of chronic low back pain patients. *Clinical Journal of Pain, 1,* 69-74.

Allan, G. (1993). Social structure and relationships. In S. Duck (Ed.), *Social context and relationships* (pp. 1-25). Newbury Park, CA: Sage.

Allen, B. (1976). *Interaction processes between the able bodied and persons confined to wheelchairs.* Unpublished manuscript, University of Western Ontario, London.

Altschuler, J. (1993). Gender and illness: Implications for family therapy. *Journal of Family Therapy, 15,* 381-401.

American Psychiatric Association. (1987). *Diagnostic and statistical manual of mental disorders* (3rd ed., rev.). Washington, DC: Author.

Anderson, B., & Coyne, J. C. (1990). Miscarried helping in the families of children and adolescents with chronic disease. In J. H. Johnson & S. H. Johnson (Eds.), *Advances in child health psychology: Proceedings of the Florida Conference* (pp. 167-177). Gainesville: University of Florida Press.

Anderson, C. M., Griffin, S., Rossi, A., Pagonis, I., Holder, D. P., & Treiber, R. A. (1986). A comparative study of the impact of education vs. process groups for families of patients with affective disorders. *Family Process, 25,* 185-205.

Anderson, M. P. (1983). Psychological disorders: Goals, treatments, and outcomes. In L. H. Peterson (Ed.), *Cardiovascular rehabilitation: A comprehensive approach* (pp. 118-146). New York: Macmillan.

Antonucci, T. C., & Jackson, J. S. (1990). The role of reciprocity in social support. In B. R. Sarason, I. G. Sarason, & G. R. Pierce (Eds.), *Social support: An interactional view* (pp. 173-198). New York: John Wiley.

Argyle, M., & Henderson, M. (1984). The rules of friendship. *Journal of Social and Personal Relationships, 1,* 211-237.

Argyle, M. (1975). *Bodily communication.* London: Methuen.

Atkins, C. J., Kaplan, R. M., & Toshima, M. T. (1991). Close relationships in the epidemiology of cardiovascular disease. In W. H. Jones & D. Perlman (Eds.), *Advances in personal relationships* (Vol. 3, pp. 207-231). London: J. Kingsley.

Babchuk, N. (1965). Primary friends and kin: A study of associations of middle-class couples. *Social Forces, 43,* 483-495.

Banfield, E. C. (1958). *The moral basis of a backward society.* Glencoe, IL: Free Press.

Baron, R. A. (1988). Negative effects of destructive criticism: Impact on conflict, self-efficacy, and task performance. *Journal of Applied Psychology, 73,* 199-207.

Barr, J. (1993). *Social support for head injured individuals and their family caregivers.* Unpublished master's thesis, Dalhousie University, Halifax, Nova Scotia.

Bar-Tal, D. (1984). American study of helping behavior. In E. Staub, D. Bar-Tal, J. Karylowski, & J. Reykowski (Eds.), *Development and maintenance of pro-social behavior* (pp. 5-27). New York: Plenum.

Bar-Tal, D., Zohar, Y. B., Greenberg, M. S., & Hermon, M. (1977). Reciprocity in relationships between donor and recipient and between harm doer and victim. *Sociometry, 40,* 293-298.

Baucom, D. H. (1987). Attribution in distressed relations: How can we explain them? In D. Perlman & S. Duck (Eds.), *Intimate relationships:*

Development, dynamics, and deterioration (pp. 177-206). Newbury Park, CA: Sage.

Baxter, L. A. (1990). Dialectical contradictions in relationship development. *Journal of Social and Personal Relationships, 7,* 69-88.

Baxter, L. A. (1993). The social side of personal relationships: A dialectical perspective. In S. Duck (Ed.), *Social context and relationships* (pp. 139-165). Newbury Park, CA: Sage.

Baxter, L. A. (1994). A dialogic approach to relational maintenance. In D. J. Canary & L. Stafford (Eds.), *Communication and relational maintenance* (pp. 233-254). New York: Academic Press.

Baxter, L. A., & Widenmann, S. (1993). Revealing and not revealing the status of romantic relationships to social networks. *Journal of Social and Personal Relationships, 10,* 321-338.

Bean, G., Cooper, S., Alpert, R., & Kipnis, D. (1980). Coping mechanisms of cancer patients. A study of 33 patients receiving chemotherapy. *CA-A, Cancer Journal for Clinicians, 30,* 256-259.

Belgrave, F. Z. (1984). The effectiveness of strategies for increasing social interaction with a physically disabled person. *Journal of Applied Social Psychology, 14,* 147-161.

Berkman, L. F. (1985). The relationship of social networks and social support to morbidity and mortality. In S. Cohen & S. L. Syme (Eds.), *Social support and health* (pp. 241-262). San Francisco: Academic Press.

Berkman, L. F., & Syme, S. L. (1979). Social networks, host resistance and mortality: A nine year follow-up of Alameda County residents. *American Journal of Epidemiology, 109,* 186-204.

Bigelow, B. J., & LaGaipa, J. J. (1975). Children's written descriptions of friendships: A multidimensional analysis. *Developmental Psychology, 11,* 857-858.

Billings, A., & Moos, R. H. (1981). The role of coping responses and social resources in attenuating the stress of life events. *Journal of Behavioral Medicine, 4,* 157-189.

Billings, A., & Moos, R. H. (1984). Coping stress and social resources among adults with unipolar depression. *Journal of Personality and Social Psychology, 46,* 157-189.

Binger, C. M., Ablin, A. R., Feverstein, R. C., Kushna, J. H., Zoger, S., & Mikkelson, C. (1969). Childhood leukemia: Emotional impact on patient and family. *New England Journal of Medicine, 280,* 414-418.

Blaxter, M. (1976). *The meaning of disability.* London: Heineman.

Block, A. R., Kremer, E. F., & Gaylor, M. (1980). Behavioral treatment of chronic pain: The spouse as a discriminative cue for pain behavior. *Pain, 9,* 143-252.

Bolger, N., DeLongis, A., Kessler, R., & Schilling, E. (1989). Effects of daily stress on negative mood. *Journal of Personality and Social Psychology, 57,* 808-818.

Borkman, T. (1990). Self-help groups at the turning point: Emerging egalitarian alliances with the formal health care system? *American Journal of Community Psychology, 18,* 321-332.

Bozeman, M. F., Orbach, C. E., & Sutherland, A. M. (1955). Psychological impact of cancer and its treatment—III: The adaptation of mothers to threatened loss of their children through leukemia. Part I. *Cancer, 8,* 1-19.

Braiker, H. B., & Kelley, H. H. (1979). Conflict in the development of close relationships. In R. I. Burgess & T. L. Huston (Eds.), *Social exchange in developing relationships* (pp. 135-168). New York: Academic Press.

Braverman, S. (1983). The relationship of social supports to health. *Canadian Family Physician, 29,* 559-569.

Brent, R. S. (1982). Community and institutional social spaces. *Therapeutic Recreation Journal, 16,* 41-48.

Brickman, P., & Bulman, R. J. (1977). Pleasure and pain in social comparison. In J. M. Suls & R. L. Miller (Eds.), *Social comparison processes: Theoretical and empirical perspectives* (pp. 149-186). Washington, DC: Hemisphere.

Broadhead, W. S., Kaplan, B. H., James, S. A., Wagner, E. H., Schoenbach, V. S., Grimson, R., Heyden, S., Tibbin, G., & Gehebach, S. H. (1983). The epidemiologic evidence for a relationship between social support and health. *American Journal of Epidemiology, 117,* 521-537.

Broese van Groenou, M., van Sonderen, E., & Ormel, J. (1990). Test-retest reliability of personal network delineation. In C. P. M. Knipscheer & T. C. Antonucci (Eds.), *Social network research* (pp. 121-136). Amsterdam: Swets & Zeitlinger.

Brown, G. W., & Harris, T. D. (1978). *Social origins of depression: A study of psychiatric disorder in women.* New York: Free Press.

Brown, J. S., & Giesy, B. (1986). Marital status of persons with spinal cord injury. *Social Science and Medicine, 23,* 313-322.

Brownell, K. D., Heckerman, C. L., Westlake, R. J., Hayes, S. C., & Monti, P. M. (1978). The effect of couples training and partner cooperativeness in the behavioral treatment of obesity. *Behavior Research and Therapy, 16,* 323-333.

Brownell, K. D., & Stunkard, A. J. (1981). Couples training, pharmacotherapy, and behavior therapy in the treatment of obesity. *Archives of General Psychiatry, 38,* 1224-1229.

Bullock, R. C., Siegal, R., Weissman, M. M., & Paykel, E. S. (1972). The weeping wife: Marital relations of depressed women. *Journal of Marriage and the Family, 34,* 488-495.

Burman, B., & Margolin, G. (1992). Analysis of the association between marital relationships and health problems: An interactional perspective. *Psychological Bulletin, 112,* 39-63.

Cade, B., & O'Hanlon, W. H. (1993). *A brief guide to brief therapy.* New York: Norton.

Caldwell, M. A., & Peplau, L. A. (1982). Sex differences in same sex friendships. *Sex Roles, 8,* 721-732.

Campbell, T. (1986). Family's impact on health: A critical review. *Family Systems Medicine, 4,* 135-323.

Caplan, G. (1974). *Support systems and community mental health: Lectures on concept development.* New York: Behavioral Publications.

Carney, R. M., Rich, M. W., teVelde, A., Saini, J., Clark, K., & Jaffe, A. S. (1987). Major depressive disorder in coronary artery disease. *American Journal of Cardiology, 60,* 1273-1275.

Charmaz, K. (1991). *Good days, bad days: The self in chronic illness and disability.* New Brunswick, NJ: Rutgers University Press.

Christie-Seely, J. (Ed.). (1984). *Working with the family in primary care.* New York: Praeger.

Clark, M. S., & Mills, J. (1979). Interpersonal attraction in exchange and communal relationships. *Journal of Personality and Social Psychology, 37,* 12-24.

Clark, M. S., & Reiss, H. T. (1988). Interpersonal processes in close relationships. *Annual Review of Psychology, 39,* 609-672.

Cobb, S. (1976). Social support as a moderator of life stress. *Psychosomatic Medicine, 38,* 300-314.

Cohen, S., & McKay, G. (1983). Social support, stress, and the buffering hypothesis: A theoretical analysis. In A. Baum, J. E. Singer, & S. E. Taylor (Eds.), *Handbook of psychology and health* (Vol. 4, pp. 253-267). Hillsdale, NJ: Lawrence Erlbaum.

Cohen, S., Mermelstein, R., Kamarck, T., & Hoberman, H. N. (1985). Measuring the functional components of social support. In I. G. Sarason & B. R. Sarason (Eds.), *Social support: Theory, research and application* (pp. 3-23). Dordrecht, The Netherlands: Martinus Nijhoff.

Cohen, S., & Wills, T. A. (1985). Stress, social support and the buffering hypothesis. *Psychological Bulletin, 98,* 310-357.

Cole, P. (1974). Morbidity in the United States. In C. L. Erhardt & J. E. Berlin (Eds.), *Mortality and morbidity in the United States* (pp. 65-104). Cambridge, MA: Harvard University Press.

Conrad, P. (1990). Qualitative research on chronic illness: A commentary on method and conceptual development. *Social Science and Medicine, 30,* 1257-1263.

Cook, S., & Makas, E. (1979). *Why some of my best friends are disabled! A study of the interaction between disabled people and nondisabled rehabilitation professionals.* Unpublished manuscript, George Washington University, Washington, DC.

Coyne, J. C. (1985). Toward a theory of frames and reframing: The social nature of frames. *Journal of Marital and Family Therapy, 11,* 337-344.

Coyne, J. C. (1987). The concept of empowerment in strategic therapy. *Psychotherapy, 24,* 539-545.

Coyne, J. C., Aldwin, C., & Lazarus, R. C. (1981). Depression and coping in stressful episodes. *Journal of Abnormal Psychology, 90,* 439-447.

Coyne, J. C., & Anderson, B. A. (1988). The "psychosomatic family" reconsidered: Diabetes in context. *Journal of Marital and Family Therapy, 14,* 113-124.

Coyne, J. C., & Anderson, B. A. (1989). The "psychosomatic family," II: Recalling a defective model and looking ahead. *Journal of Marital and Family Therapy, 15,* 139-148.

Coyne, J. C., & DeLongis, A. M. (1986). Going beyond social support: The role of social relationships in adaptation. *Journal of Consulting and Clinical Psychology, 54,* 454-460.

Coyne, J. C., & Downey, G. (1991). Social factors and psychopathology: Stress, social support and coping processes. *Annual Review of Psychology, 42,* 410-425.

Coyne, J. C., Downey, G., & Boergers, J. (1992). Depression in families: A systems perspective. In D. Cicchetti & S. L. Toth (Eds.), *Developmental approaches to the affective disorders: Rochester Symposium on Developmental Psychopathology, Vol. 4* (pp. 211-249). Rochester, NY: University of Rochester Press.

Coyne, J. C., Ellard, J. H., & Smith, D. A. (1990). Social support, interdependence, and the dilemmas of helping. In B. R. Sarason, I. G. Sarason, & G. R. Pierce (Eds.), *Social support: An interactional view* (pp. 129-149). New York: John Wiley.

Coyne, J. C., & Fiske, V. (1992). Couples coping with chronic illness. In T. J. Akamatsu, J. C. Crowther, S. C. Hobfoll, & M. A. P. Stevens (Eds.), *Family health psychology* (pp. 129-149). Washington, DC: Hemisphere.

Coyne, J. C., & Smith, D. A. F. (1991). Couples coping with myocardial infarction: I. A contextual perspective on wives' distress. *Journal of Personality and Social Psychology, 6,* 404-412.

Coyne, J. C., & Smith, D. A. F. (1994). Couples coping with myocardial infarction: Contextual perspectives on patient self-efficacy. *Journal of Family Psychology, 8,* 1-13.

Coyne, J. C., & Sonnega, J. (1994, July). *Emotional regulation in couples coping with cardiovascular disease.* Paper presented at the International Society for Research on Emotion, Cambridge, UK.

Coyne, J. C., Wortman, C., & Lehman, D. (1988). The other side of support: Emotional overinvolvement and miscarried helping. In B. H. Gottlieb (Ed.), *Marshalling social support: Formats, processes, and effects* (pp. 309-330). Newbury Park, CA: Sage.

Crewe, N. M., Athelstan, G. T., & Krumberger. J. (1979). Spinal cord injury: A comparison of pre-injury and post-injury marriages. *Archives of Physical Medicine and Rehabilitation, 60,* 252-256.

Croog, H. S., & Levine, S. (1977). *The heart patient recovers: Social and psychological factors.* New York: Human Sciences Press.

Croog, H. S., & Levine, S. (1982). *Life after a heart attack: Social and psychological factors eight years later.* New York: Human Sciences Press.

Cutrona, C. E., & Russell, D. W. (1987). The provisions of relationships and adaptation to stress. In D. Perlman & W. Jones (Eds.), *Advances in personal relationships* (Vol. 1, pp. 37-67). Greenwich, CT: JAI.

Dakof, G. A., & Taylor, S. E. (1990). Victim's perception of social support: What is helpful from whom? *Journal of Personality and Social Psychology, 58,* 80-89.

Davis, F. (1961). Deviance disavowal: The management of strained interactions between the visibly handicapped. *Social Problems, 9,* 120-132.

Davis-Ali, S., Frazier, P., & Krasnoff, A. (1994, July). *Coping and adjustment among patients and their significant others.* Paper presented at the Seventh International Conference on Personal Relationships, Groningen, The Netherlands.

Dean, A., & Linn, N. (1977). The stress buffering role of social support: Problems and prospects for systematic investigation. *Journal of Nervous and Mental Disease, 165,* 403-417.

de Jong-Gierveld, J. (1988, July). Symposium overview. In J. de Jong-Gierveld (Convenor), *Life changes and the network of personal relationships.* Symposium conducted at the Fourth International Conference on Personal Relationships, Vancouver, British Columbia, Canada.

Dembo, T., Leviton, G. L., & Wright, B. (1975). Adjustment to misfortune. *Rehabilitation Psychology, 22,* 1-91.

Derogatis, L. R. (1986). The Psychosocial Adjustment to Illness Scale (PAIS). *Journal of Psychosomatic Research, 30,* 77-91.

Devins, G. M., & Seland, T. P. (1987). Emotional impact of multiple sclerosis: Recent findings and suggestions for future research. *Psychological Bulletin, 101,* 363-375.

DiMatteo, M. R., & Hays, R. (1981). Social support and serious illness. In B. H. Gottlieb (Ed.), *Social networks and social support* (pp. 117-148). Beverly Hills, CA: Sage.

Dindia, K., & Canary, D. J. (1993). Definitions and theoretical perspectives on maintaining relationships. *Journal of Social and Personal Relationships, 10,* 163-173.

Doherty, W. J., & Baird, M. (1983). *Family therapy and family medicine: Towards the primary care of families.* New York: Guilford.

Duck, S. W. (1981). Toward a research map for the study of relationship breakdown. In S. W. Duck & R. Gilmour (Eds.), *Personal relationships 3: Personal relationships in disorder* (pp. 1-29). London: Sage.

Duck, S. W. (Ed.). (1988). *Handbook of personal relationships.* New York: John Wiley.

Duck, S. W. (1991). *Understanding relationships.* New York: Guilford.

Duck, S. (1993a). Volume preface. In S. Duck (Ed.), *Social context and relationships* (pp. ix-xiv). Newbury Park, CA: Sage.

Duck, S. (Ed.). (1993b). *Social context and relationships.* Newbury Park, CA: Sage.

Duck, S. (1994). *Meaningful relationships: Talking, sense, and relating.* Thousand Oaks, CA: Sage.

Duck, S., & Sants, H. (1983). On the origin of the species: Are personal relationships really interpersonal states? *Journal of Social and Clinical Psychology, 1,* 27-41.

Dunkel-Schetter, C., Folkman, S., & Lazarus, R. (1987). Correlates of social support receipt. *Journal of Personality and Social Psychology, 53,* 71-80.

Dunkel-Schetter, C., & Skokan, L. A. (1990). Determinants of social support provision in personal relationships. *Journal of Social and Personal Relationships, 7,* 437-450.

Dunkel-Schetter, C., & Wortman, C. B. (1982). The interpersonal dynamics of cancer: Problems in social relationships and their impact on the patient. In H. S. Friedman & M. R. DiMatteo (Eds.), *Interpersonal issues in health care* (pp. 69-100). New York: Academic Press.

Dunn, M. (1975). Psychological intervention in a spinal cord injury center: An introduction. *Rehabilitation Psychology, 22,* 165-178.

Dura, J. R., & Beck, S. R. (1988). A comparison of family functioning when mothers have chronic pain. *Pain, 35,* 79-90.

Eckenrode, J. (1991). *The social context of coping.* New York: Plenum.

Eisenberg, M., Griggins, C., & Duval, R. (1982). *Disabled people as second class citizens.* New York: Springer-Verlag.

Environics Research Group Ltd. (1989). *The needs and attitudes of disabled Ontarians.* Toronto: Office for Disabled Persons, Province of Ontario, Canada.

Evans, B. L., & Northwood, L. K. (1981). Interpersonal relations in adjustment to stroke. *International Journal of Rehabilitation Research, 4,* 534-536.

Fichten, C. S., & Amsel, R. (1986). Trait attributions about physically disabled university students: Circumplex analysis and methodological issues. *Journal of Applied Social Psychology, 16,* 410-427.

Fichten, C. S., Robillard, K., Tagalakis, V., & Amsel, R. (1991). Casual interaction between college students with various disabilities and their nondisabled peers: The internal dialogue. *Rehabilitation Psychology, 36,* 3-20.

Fisch, R., Weakland, J. H., & Segal, L. (1984). *The tactics of change.* San Francisco: Jossey-Bass.

Fischer, C. (1982). *To dwell among friends.* Chicago: University of Chicago Press.

Fisher, B., & Galler, R. (1988). Friendship and fairness: How disability affects friendship. In M. Fine & A. Asch (Eds.), *Women with disabilities:*

Essays in psychology, culture, and politics (pp. 172-194). Philadelphia: Temple University Press.

Fisher, J. D., & Nadler, A. (1974). The effect of similarity between donor and recipient on reactions to aid. *Journal of Applied Social Psychology, 4*, 230-243.

Fiske, V., Coyne, J. C., & Smith, D. A. (1991). Couples coping with myocardial infarction: An empirical reconsideration of the role of over-protectiveness. *Journal of Family Psychology, 5*, 4-20.

Flor, H., Kerns, R. D., & Turk, D. C. (1987). The role of spouse reinforcement, perceived pain, and activity levels of chronic pain patients. *Journal of Psychosomatic Research, 31*, 251-259.

Flor, H., Turk, D. C., & Scholz, O. B. (1987). Impact of chronic pain on the spouse: Marital, emotional, and physical consequences. *Journal of Psychosomatic Research, 31*, 63-71.

Floyd, K. (1994, July). *Gender and intimacy among same-sex friends and same-sex siblings*. Paper presented at the Seventh International Conference on Personal Relationships, Groningen, The Netherlands.

Foa, U. G., & Foa, E. B. (1974). *Societal structures of the mind*. Springfield, IL: Charles C Thomas.

Fontana, A. F., Kerns, R. D., Rosenburg, R. L., & Colonese, K. L. (1989). Support, stress, and recovery from coronary heart disease: A longitudinal causal model. *Health Psychology, 8*, 175-193.

Fordyce, W. E. (1976). *Behavioral methods for chronic pain and illness*. St. Louis, MO: C. V. Mosby.

Francis, J., Lascelles, M. A., Cappon, P., & Brunelli, G. (1993). Health care policy and out-reach rehabilitation in Canada. *Canadian Journal of Rehabilitation, 6*, 203-207.

Frank, R. G., Beck, N. C., Parker, J. C., Kashani, J. H., Elliott, T. R., Haut, A. E., Smith, E., Atwood, C., Brownlee-Duffeck, M., & Kay, D. R. (1988). Depression in rheumatoid arthritis. *Journal of Rheumatology, 15*, 920-925.

Frank, R. G., Wonderlich, S. A., Corcoran, J. R., Umlauf, R. L., Ashkanazi, G. H., Brownlee-Duffeck, M. B., & Wilson, R. (1986). Interpersonal response to spinal cord injury. *Journal of Social and Clinical Psychology, 4*, 447-460.

French, R. D. (1984). The long term relationships of marked people. In E. E. Jones, A. Farina, A. M. Hastorf, M. Markus, D. T. Miller, & R. A. Scott (Eds.), *Social stigma: The psychology of marked relationships* (pp. 255-294). New York: Freeman.

Gilligan, C. (1982). *In a different voice: Psychological theory and women's development*. Cambridge, MA: Harvard University Press.

Gillis, C. (1984). Reducing family stress during and after coronary artery bypass surgery. *Nursing Clinics of North America, 19*, 1103-1111.

Glick, I. O., Weiss, R. S., & Parkes, C. M. (1974). *The first years of bereavement*. New York: John Wiley.

Goffman, E. (1963). *Stigma: Notes on the management of a soiled identity.* Englewood Cliffs, NJ: Prentice Hall.

Gonzalez, S., Steinglass, P., & Reiss, D. (1989). Putting the illness in its place: Discussion groups for families with chronic medical illnesses. *Family Process, 28,* 69-87.

Gooderham, M. (1993, December 4). Learning how to die—Dennis Kaye will let Lou Gehrig's Disease take its course. *Toronto Globe and Mail,* p. D5.

Gordon, M., & Downing, H. (1978). A multivariate test of the Bott hypotheses in an urban setting. *Journal of Marriage and the Family, 40,* 585-593.

Gore, S., & Colton, M. E. (1991). Gender, stress, and distress: Social-relational influences. In J. Eckenrode (Ed.), *The social context of coping* (pp. 139-163). New York: Plenum.

Gottlieb, B. H. (1981). *Social networks and social support.* Beverly Hills, CA: Sage.

Gottlieb, B. H. (1988). Marshalling social support: The state of the art in research and practice. In B. H. Gottlieb (Ed.), *Marshalling social support: Formats, processes, and effects* (pp. 11-52). Newbury Park, CA: Sage.

Gottlieb, B. H. (1989). A contextual perspective on stress in family care of the elderly. *Canadian Psychology, 30,* 596-607.

Gottlieb, B. H. (1992). Quandries in translating support concepts to intervention. In H. O. F. Veiel & U. Baumann (Eds.), *The series in clinical and community psychology* (pp. 293-309). New York: Hemisphere.

Gottlieb, B. H. (in press). Stress and coping processes in close relationships. In J. Eckenrode (Ed.), *The social context of stress.* New York: Plenum.

Gottlieb, B. H., & Wagner, F. (1991). Stress and support processes in close relationships. In J. Eckenrode (Ed.), *The social context of coping* (pp. 165-188). New York: Plenum.

Gottman, J. M. (1991). Predicting the longitudinal course of marriages. *Journal of Marital and Family Therapy, 17,* 3-7.

Government of Canada. (1981). *Obstacles.* Special Committtee on the Disabled and Handicapped, Third Report (Supply and Services Canada Cat. No. XC 2-321/5-03E). Ottawa: Author.

Government of Canada. (1991). *The national strategy for the integration of persons with disabilities.* (Supply and Services Canada Cat. No. S2-217/1991). Ottawa: Author.

Guay, J. (1982). The social network of the ex-patient. *Canada's Mental Health, 30,* 22.

Haley, J. (1973). *Uncommon therapy: The psychiatric techniques of Milton H. Erikson, M.D.* New York: Norton.

Hamilton, G. A. (1990). Recovery from myocardial infarction in women. *Cardiology, 77*(Suppl. 2), 58-70.

Hammer, M. (1983). "Core" and "extended" social networks in relation to health and illness. *Social Science & Medicine, 17*, 405-411.

Hansson, R. O., Jones, W. H., & Carpenter, B. N. (1984). Relational competence and social support. In P. Shaver (Ed.), *Review of personality and social psychology* (Vol. 5, pp. 265-284). Beverly Hills, CA: Sage.

Hansson, R. O., Jones, W. H., & Fletcher W. L. (1990). Troubled relationships in later life: Implications for support. *Journal of Social and Personal Relationships, 7*, 451-453.

Harker, B. L. (1972). Cancer and communication problems: A personal experience. *Psychiatry in Medicine, 3*, 163-171.

Hartup, W. W. (1975). The origins of friendship. In M. Lewis & L. A. Rosenblum (Eds.), *Friendship and peer relations* (pp. 11-26). New York: John Wiley.

Hatfield, E., Traupmann, J., Sprecher, S., Utne, M., & Hay, J. (1984). Behavioral interdependence: Social exchange. In W. Ickes (Ed.), *Compatible and incompatible relationships* (pp. 1-27). New York: Springer-Verlag.

Hays, R. B. (1988). Friendship. In S. W. Duck (Ed.), *Handbook of personal relationships* (pp. 391-408). Chichester, UK: John Wiley.

Hegelson, V. S. (1994, July). *Social support and adjustment to breast cancer.* Paper presented at the Seventh International Conference on Personal Relationships, Groningen, The Netherlands.

Heineman, A. W., & Shontz, F. C. (1984). Adjustment following disability: Representative case studies. *Rehabilitation Counselling Bulletin, 28*, 1-14.

Henderson, K. A., & Allen, K. R. (1990, May). *The ethic of care: Leisure possibilities and constraints for women.* Paper presented at the Canadian Congress on Leisure Research, Waterloo, Ontario.

Henderson, K. A., & Bedini, L. A., & Schuler, R. (1993, May). *The negotiation of leisure constraints by women with disabilities.* Paper presented at the Canadian Congress on Leisure Research, Winnipeg, Manitoba.

Hendrick, S. (1986). An arranged marriage. *Contemporary Psychology, 31*, 334-336.

Henrich, E., & Kriegel, L. (Eds.). (1961). *Experiments in survival.* New York: Association for the Aid of Crippled Children.

Heusemann, L. R., & Levinger, G. (1976). Incremental exchange theory: A formal model for progression in dyadic interaction. In L. Berkowitz & E. Walster (Eds.), *Advances in experimental social psychology* (Vol. 9, pp. 192-229). New York: Academic Press.

Hilbert, R. A. (1984). The acultural dimension of pain: Flawed reality construction and the problem of meaning. *Social Problems, 31*, 365-378.

Hilbourne, J. (1973). On disabling the normal. *British Journal of Social Work, 2*, 497-507.

Hinde, R. A. (1981). The bases of a science of interpersonal relationships. In S. W. Duck & R. Gilmour (Eds.), *Personal relationships 1: Studying personal relationships* (pp. 1-22). London: Academic Press.

Hirsch, B. (1980). Natural support systems in coping with life changes. *American Journal of Community Psychology, 8,* 159-173.

Hobfoll, S. E. (1989). Conservation of resources: A new attempt at conceptualizing stress. *American Psychologist, 44,* 513-524.

Hoebel, F. C. (1977). Coronary artery disease and family interaction: A study of risk factor modification. In P. Watzlawick & J. Weakland (Eds.), *The interactional view* (pp. 136-151). New York: Norton.

Hoffman, L. (1975). *Foundations of family therapy: A conceptual framework for systems change.* New York: Basic Books.

Holahan, C. J., & Moos, R. H. (1987). Personal and contextual determinants of coping strategies. *Journal of Personality and Social Psychology, 52,* 946-955.

Honigmann, J. J. (1968). Perspectives on the atomistic type society: Interpersonal relations in atomistic communities. *Human Organization, 27,* 220-229.

Hooley, J. M., Orley, J., & Teasdale, J. D. (1986). Levels of expressed emotion and relapse in depression. *British Journal of Psychiatry, 148,* 642-647.

Hooley, J. M., & Teasdale, J. D. (1989). Predictors of relapse in unipolar depressives: Expressed emotion, marital distress, and perceived criticism. *Journal of Abnormal Psychology, 98,* 229-235.

House, J., Landis, K. R., & Umberson, D. (1988). Social relationships and health. *Science, 141,* 540-545.

Hutchison, P., & McGill, J. (1992). *Leisure, integration and community.* Concord, Ontario: Leisurability Publications Ltd.

Iso-Ahola, S. E. (1986). A theory of substitutability of leisure behavior. *Leisure Sciences, 8,* 367-389.

Jaffe, D. T., & Jordon-Marsh, M. (1983). Styles of couple response to a health behavior change program. *Family Systems Medicine, 1,* 37-46.

Janssen, M., Philipsen, H., & Halfens, R. (1990, July). *Personal networks of chronically ill people.* Paper presented at the Fifth International Conference on Personal Relationships, Oxford University, Oxford, UK.

Jensen, M. P., Turner, J. A., Romano, J. M., & Karoly, P. (1991). Coping with chronic pain: A critical review of the literature. *Pain, 47,* 249-283.

Joffe, R. T., Lippert, G. P., Gray, T. A., Sawa, G., & Horvath, Z. (1987). Mood disorder and multiple sclerosis. *Archives of Neurology, 44,* 376-378.

Johnson, C. L. (1983). Fairweather friends and rainy day kin: An anthropological analysis of old age friendships in the United States. *Urban Anthropology, 12,* 103-123.

Jones, E. E., Farina, A. H., Hastorf, A. H., Markus, H., Miller, D. T., Scott, R. A., & French, R. D. (1984). *Social stigma: The psychology of marked relationships.* New York: Freeman.

Jones, R. A. (1970). Volunteering for help: The effects of choice, dependence, and anticipated departure. *Journal of Personality and Social Psychology, 14,* 121-129.

Jones, W. H., Hobbs, S. A., & Hockenbury, D. (1982). Loneliness and social skill deficits. *Journal of Personality and Social Psychology, 42,* 682-689.

Keefe, F. J., Brown, G. K., Wallston, K. A., & Caldwell, D. S. (1989). Coping with rheumatoid arthritis: Catastrophizing as a maladaptive strategy. *Pain, 37,* 51-56.

Kelley, H. H. (1983). Love and commitment. In H. H. Kelley, E. Berscheid, A. Christensen, J. H. Harvey, T. L. Huston, G. Levinger, E. McClintock, L. A. Peplau, & D. L. Peterson (Eds.), *Close relationships* (pp. 265-314). New York: Freeman.

Kelley, H. H., & Thibaut, J. W. (1978). *Interpersonal relations: A theory of interdependence.* New York: John Wiley.

Kerns, R. D., & Turk, D. C. (1985). *Health, illness, and families: A lifespan perspective.* New York: John Wiley.

Kiecolt-Glaser, J. K., Dyer, C. S., & Shuttleworth, E. C. (1988). Upsetting social interactions and distress among Alzheimer's disease family caregivers: A replication and extension. *American Journal of Community Psychology, 16,* 825-837.

Kiecolt-Glaser, J. K., Glaser, R., Willinger, D., Stout, J., Messick, G., Sheppard, S., Ricker, D., Romisher, S. C., Briner, W., Bonnell, G., & Donnerberg, R. (1985). Psycho-social enhancement of immunocompetence in a geriatric population. *Health Psychology, 4,* 25-41.

Kimmel, D. C. (1979). Relationship initiation and development: A life-span developmental approach. In R. L. Burgess & T. L. Huston (Eds.), *Social exchange in developing relationships* (pp. 351-377). New York: Academic Press.

Kinney, T., & Coyle, K. (1989). *Predicting life satisfaction among physically disabled adults: Leisure's contribution* (Unpublished Rep. 062-00). Philadelphia: Temple University, Department of Recreation and Leisure Studies.

Kleck, R. E. (1968). Physical stigma and non-verbal cues emitted in face-to-face interaction. *Human Relations, 21,* 119-128.

Kleck, R. E. (1969). Physical stigma and task-oriented interaction. *Human Relations, 22,* 53-60.

Kleck, R., Ono, H., & Hastorf, A. H. (1966). The effects of physical deviance upon face-to-face interaction. *Human Relations, 19,* 425-436.

Klein, R., & Milardo, R. M. (1993). Third-party influences on the management of personal relationships. In S. Duck (Ed.), *Social context and relationships* (pp. 55-77). Newbury Park, CA: Sage.

Kramlinger, K. G., Swanson, D. W., & Maruta, T. (1983). Are patients with chronic pain depressed? *American Journal of Psychiatry, 140,* 747-749.

Kübler-Ross, E. (1969). *On death and dying.* New York: Macmillan.

Ladieu-Leviton, G., Adler, D. L., & Dembo, T. (1948). Studies in adjustment to visible injuries: Social acceptance of the injured. *Journal of Social Issues, 4*(14), 55-61.

LaGaipa, J. J. (1977). Testing a multidimensional approach to friendship. In S. Duck (Ed.), *Theory and practice in interpersonal attraction* (pp. 249-270). London: Academic Press.

LaGaipa, J. J. (1984, July). *Burnout in the informal social network of cancer patients.* Paper presented at the Second International Conference on Personal Relationships, Madison, WI.

Lam, D. H., & Power, M. J. (1991). Social support in a general practice elderly sample. *International Journal of Geriatric Psychology, 6,* 89-93.

Lazarus, R. S. (1966). *Psychological stress and coping process.* New York: McGraw-Hill.

Lazarus, R. S., & Folkman, S. (1984). *Stress, appraisal, and coping.* New York: Springer-Verlag.

Leff, J. P., & Vaughn, C. E. (1980). The interaction of life events and relatives' expressed emotion in schizophrenia and depressive neurosis. *British Journal of Psychiatry, 136,* 146-153.

Lehman, D. R., Ellard, J. H., & Wortman, C. B. (1986). Social support for the bereaved: Recipients' and providers' perspectives on what is helpful. *Journal of Clinical and Consulting Psychology, 54,* 438-446.

Leventhal, G. W. (1980). What should be done with equity theory? New approaches to the study of fairness in social relationships. In K. J. Gergen, M. S. Greenberg, & R. Willis (Eds.), *Social exchange: Advances in theory and research* (pp. 22-55). New York: Plenum.

Levy, D. M. (1943). *Maternal overprotection.* New York: Columbia University Press.

Lewin, K. (1948). The background of conflict in marriage. In G. W. Lewin (Ed.), *Resolving social conflicts* (pp. 84-102). New York: Harper.

Lichtenstein, E., Glasgow, R. E., & Abrams, D. B. (1986). Social support in smoking cessation: In search of effective interventions. *Behavior Therapy, 17,* 605-619.

Lin, N., Ensel, W. M., Simeone, R. S., & Kuo, W. (1979). Social support, stressful life events and illness: A model and empirical test. *Journal of Health and Social Behavior, 20,* 108-119.

Lopata, H. Z., Heinemann, G. D., & Baum, J. (1982). Loneliness: Antecedents and coping strategies in the lives of widows. In L. A. Peplau & D. Perlman (Eds.), *Loneliness: A sourcebook of current theory, research and therapy* (pp. 310-326). New York: John Wiley.

Love, A. W. (1987). Depression in chronic low back pain patients: Diagnostic efficiency of three self-report questionnaires. *Journal of Clinical Psychology, 43,* 84-89.

Lowry, M. R., & Atcherson, E. (1979). Characteristics of patients with depressive disorder on entry into home hemodialysis. *Journal of Nervous and Mental Disease, 167,* 748-751.

Lynch, J. J. (1977). *The broken heart: The medical consequences of loneliness.* New York: Basic Books.

Lyons, R. (1986). *The impact of chronic illness on activity patterns and friendships* (Research report). Ottawa: Fitness & Lifestyle Research Institute.

Lyons, R. (1987). Leisure adjustment to chronic illness and disability. *Journal of Leisurability, 14*(2), 4-10.

Lyons, R. (1991). The effects of acquired illness and disability on friendships. In D. Perlman & W. Jones (Eds.), *Advances in personal relationships* (Vol. 3, pp. 223-277). London: J. Kingsley.

Lyons, R. (1993a). Research on relationships coping with stressful life events: An interview with Ben Gottlieb and James Coyne. *International Society for the Study of Personal Relationships Bulletin, 10*(1), 11-14.

Lyons, R. (1993b). *The energy crunch: Relationship and support experiences of mothers with chronic illness.* Paper presented at Studying Human Lived Experience: Symbolic and Ethnographic Research '93, University of Waterloo, Waterloo, Ontario.

Lyons, R., & Langille, L. (1995). *Coping shared experiences and mutual support: The C. F. mother's group.* Manuscript in preparation.

Lyons, R., & Meade, D. (1993a, June). *Coping and support as communal processes.* Paper presented at the Fourth Conference of the International Network on Personal Relationships, Milwaukee, WI.

Lyons, R., & Meade, D. (1993b). The energy crisis: Mothers with chronic illness. *Canadian Woman Studies, 13*(4), 34-37.

Lyons, R. F., & Meade, D. (1995). Painting a new face on relationships: Relationship remodeling in response to chronic illness. In S. Duck & J. T. Wood (Eds.), *Confronting relationship challenges* (pp. 181-210). Thousand Oaks, CA: Sage.

Lyons, R. F., & Mickelson, K. D. (1994, July). *Stressful life events and communal coping processes.* Paper presented at the Seventh International Conference on Personal Relationships, Groningen, The Netherlands.

Lyons, R., Ritvo, P., & Sullivan, M. (1992, July). *Social functioning and chronic illness: Relationship quality, friendship, and marriage.* Symposium conducted at the Sixth International Conference on Personal Relationships, Orono, ME.

Manfredo, M., & Anderson, D. (1985). The influence of activity importance and similarity on perception of recreation substitutes. *Leisure Sciences, 8,* 367-389.

Manne, S. L., & Zautra, A. J. (1989). Spouse criticism and support: Their association with coping and psychological adjustment among women with rheumatoid arthritis. *Journal of Personality and Social Psychology, 56,* 608-617.

Marinelli, R. P., & Dell Orto, A. E. (1984). *The psychological and social impact of physical disability.* New York: Springer-Verlag.

Maruta, T., Osbourne, D., Swanson, D. W., & Halling, J. M. (1981). Chronic pain patients and spouses: Marital and sexual adjustment. *Mayo Clinic Proceedings, 56,* 307-310.

Mathews, G. (1983). *Voices from the shadows: Women with disabilities speak out.* Toronto: Women's Press.

McCarthy, H. (1983). Understanding the motives of youth in transition to work: A taxonomy for rehabilitation counselors and educators. *Journal of Applied Rehabilitation Counseling, 14*(1), 52-61.

McCubbin, M. A., & Patterson, J. (1981). *Family stress and adaptation to crisis: A double ABCX model of family behavior.* Paper presented at the annual meeting of the National Council on Family Relations, Milwaukee, WI.

McDaniel, S., Hepworth, J., & Doherty, W. (1992). *Medical family therapy: A biopsychosocial approach.* New York: Basic Books.

Meade, D. (1994). *Defining support: The relational experiences of mothers with multiple sclerosis.* Unpublished master's thesis, Dalhousie University, Halifax, Nova Scotia.

Mechanic, D. (1972). Social psychologic factors affecting the presentation of bodily complants. *New England Journal of Medicine, 286,* 1132-1139.

Meichenbaum, D., & Turk, D. C. (1987). *Facilitating treatment adherence: A practitioner's guidebook.* New York: Plenum.

Merton, R. K. (1957). *Social theory and social structure.* New York: Free Press.

Michela, J. (1981). *Perceived changes in marital relationships following myocardial infarction.* Unpublished doctoral dissertation, University of California, Los Angeles.

Mickelson, K. (1993). *Chronic stressor dimensions' effects on perceived social support: A literature review.* Unpublished manuscript, Carnegie Mellon University, Pittsburgh.

Miklowitz, D. J., Goldstein, M. J., Nuechterlein, K. H., Snyder, K. S., & Mintz, J. (1988). Family factors and the course of bipolar affective disorder. *Archives of General Psychiatry, 45,* 225-231.

Milardo, R. M. (1992). Delineating social networks. *Journal of Social and Personal Relationships, 9,* 447-461.

Milardo, R., & Wellman, B. (1992). The person is social. *Journal of Social and Personal Relationships, 9,* 339-342.

Mills, J., Belgrave, F. Z., & Boyer, K. M. (1984). Reducing avoidance of social interaction with a physically disabled person by mentioning the disability following a request for aid. *Journal of Applied Social Psychology, 14*(1), 1-11.

Minden, S. L., Orav, J., & Reich, P. (1987). Depression in multiple sclerosis. *General Hospital Psychiatry, 9,* 426-434.

Mingo, F. E. (1993). *The caregiver.* Halifax, Nova Scotia: Largo.

Minnich, E. K. (1985). Friendship between women: The art of feminist biography. *Feminist Studies, 11,* 287-306.

Minuchin, S. (1974). *Families and family therapy*. Cambridge, MA: Harvard University Press.

Minuchin, S., Rosman, B. L., & Baker, L. (1978). *Psychosomatic families: Anorexia nervosa in context*. Cambridge, MA: Harvard University Press.

Monsour, M. (1992). Meanings of intimacy in cross- and same-sex friendships. *Journal of Social and Personal Relationships, 9,* 277-295.

Montgomery, B. (1993). Relationship maintenance versus relationship change: A dialectical dilemma. *Journal of Social and Personal Relationships, 10,* 205-223.

Moos, R. H., & Tsu, V. D. (1977). The crisis of physical illness. In R. H. Moos (Ed.), *Coping with physical illness* (pp. 3-21). New York: Plenum.

Morgan, D. L. (1987, May). *Who your friends really are: Reorganizing relationships in widowhood*. Paper presented at the Iowa Conference on Personal Relationships, Iowa City.

Morgan, D., & March, S. J. (1992). The impact of life events on networks of personal relationships: A comparison of widowhood and caring for a spouse with Alzheimer's disease. *Journal of Social and Personal Relationships, 9,* 563-584.

Morgan, M., Patrick, D. L., & Charlton, J. R. (1984). Social networks and psychosocial support among disabled people. *Social Science and Medicine, 19,* 489-497.

Morisky, D. E., Levine, D. M., Green, L. W., Shapiro, S., Russell, R. P., & Smith, C. R. (1983). Five year blood pressure control and mortality following health education for hypertensive patients. *American Journal of Public Health, 73,* 153-162.

Morse, J. M., & Johnson, J. L. (1991). *The illness experience: Dimensions of suffering*. Newbury Park, CA: Sage.

Murray, T. J. (1992, April). The journal of a disappointed man: A patient's perspective on multiple sclerosis. *Nova Scotia Medical Journal*, pp. 59-62.

Murstein, B. I., Cerreto, M., & MacDonald, M. G. (1977). A theory and investigation of the effect of exchange-orientation on marriage and friendship. *Journal of Marriage and the Family, 39,* 543-548.

National Center for Health Statistics. (1983). *Americans assess their health: United States, 1978* (DHHS Publication No. PHS 83-1570). Washington, DC: Government Printing Office.

National Center for Health Statistics. (1984). *Health, United States, 1984* (DHHS Publication No. PHS 85-1232). Washington, DC: Government Printing Office.

Newcomb, M. (1981). Heterosexual cohabitation relationships. In S. Duck & R. Gilmour (Eds.), *Personal relationships 1: Studying personal relationships* (pp. 131-164). London: Academic Press.

Newcomb, M., & Bentler, P. M. (1981). Marital breakdown. In S. Duck & R. Gilmour (Eds.), *Personal relationships 3: Personal relationships in disorder* (pp. 57-94). London: Sage.

Nuckolls, K. P., Cassel, J., & Kaplan, B. H. (1972). Psychosocial aspects, life crisis and the prognosis of pregnancy. *American Journal of Epidemiology, 95*, 431-441.

Notarius, C. I., & Herrick, L. R. (1988). Listener response strategies to a distressed other. *Journal of Personal and Social Relationships, 5*, 97-108.

Oddy, M. J., Humphrey, M. E., & Uttley, D. (1978). Stresses upon the relatives of head injured patients. *British Journal of Psychiatry, 133*, 507-513.

Olson, D. H., McCubbin, H. I., Barnes, H. L., Larsen, A. S., Muxan, M. J., & Wilson, M. A. (1983). *Families: What makes them work.* Beverly Hills, CA: Sage.

Olson, D. H., Sprenkle, D. H., & Russell, C. L. (1979). Circumplex model of marital and family systems: 1. Cohesion and adaptability dimensions, familiar types, and clinical applications. *Family Process, 18*, 3-27.

O'Neil, P. M. (1979). Effects of sex on subject and spouse involvement on weight loss in a behavioral treatment program: A retrospective investigation. *Addictive Behaviors, 4*, 167-178.

Pal, D. (1992). "Catch 22" for unemployed disabled adults: Ontario March of Dimes Study. *Abilities, 12*(3), 52-53.

Palisi, B. J., & Ransford, H. E. (1987). Friendship as a voluntary relationship: Evidence from national surveys. *Journal of Social and Personal Relationships, 4*, 243-259.

Parks, M., & Floyd, K. (1994, June). *Intimacy and closeness as alternatives for specifying the characteristics of friendship.* Paper presented at the annual meeting of the International Network on Personal Relationships, Iowa City, IA.

Patrick, D. L., Morgan, M., & Charlton, J. R. H. (1986). Psycho-social support and change in the health status of physically disabled people. *Social Science & Medicine, 22*, 1347-1354.

Patterson, I. (1984). Recreation and multiple sclerosis. In A. F. Simons (Ed.), *Multiple sclerosis: Psychological and social aspects* (pp. 101-114). London: Heinemann Medical Books.

Pearce, J. W., LeBow, M. D., & Orchard, J. (1981). Role of spouse involvement in the behavioral treatment of overweight women. *Journal of Consulting and Clinical Psychology, 49*, 236-244.

Pearlin, L. I. (1991). The study of coping: An overview of problems and directions. In J. Eckenrode (Ed.), *The social context of coping* (pp. 261-276). New York: Plenum.

Pearlin, L. I., & Lieberman, M. A. (1979). Social sources of emotional distress. In R. Simmons (Ed.), *Research in community and mental health* (Vol. 1, pp. 217-248). Greewich, CT: JAI.

Pearlin, L. I., Lieberman, M. A., Menaghan, E., & Mullan, J. T. (1981). The stress process. *Journal of Health and Social Behaviour, 22*, 337-356.

Pearlin, L. I., & Schooler, C. (1978). The structure of coping. *Journal of Health and Social Behaviour, 19,* 2-21.

Perlman, D. (1982). Perspectives on loneliness. In L. A. Peplau & D. Perlman (Eds.), *Loneliness: A sourcebook of current theory, research, and therapy* (pp. 1-18). New York: John Wiley.

Planalp, S., & Garvin-Doxas, K. (1994). Using mutual knowledge in conversation: Friends as experts on each other. In S. Duck (Ed.), *Dynamics of relationships* (pp. 1-26). Thousand Oaks, CA: Sage.

Pohl, C. M., & Winland-Brown, J. E. (1992). The meaning of disability in a caring environment. *Journal of Nursing Administration, 22,* 29-35.

Popkin, M. K., Callies, A. L., Lentz, R. D., Colon, E. A., & Sutherland, D. E. (1988). Prevalence of major depression, simple phobia, and other psychiatric disorders in patients with long standing Type I diabetes mellitus. *Archives of General Psychiatry, 45,* 64-68.

Porritt, D. (1979). Social support in crisis: Quantity or quality? *Social Science and Medicine, 13A,* 715-721.

Power, P. W. (1985). Family coping behaviors in chronic illness: A rehabilitation perspective. *Rehabilitation Literature, 46,* 78-83.

Radley, A. (1988). *Prospects of heart surgery.* New York: Springer-Verlag.

Ransom, D. C. (1989). Development of family therapy and family theory. In C. N. Ramsey (Ed.), *Family systems in medicine* (pp. 18-35). New York: Guilford.

Rapkin, B. D., & Stein, C. H. (1989). Defining personal networks. *American Journal of Community Psychology, 17,* 259-267.

Rausch, H. (1974). *Communication, conflict, and marriage.* San Francisco: Jossey-Bass.

Rawlins, W. K. (1992). *Friendship matters: Communication, dialectics and the life course.* Hawthorne, NY: Aldine de Gruyter.

Reed, D., McGee, D., Yano, K., & Feinleib, M. (1983). Social networks and CHD among Japanese men in Hawaii. *American Journal of Epidemiology, 117,* 384-396.

Renwick, R. (1992). *Quality of life project, Phase 1.* Toronto: University of Toronto, The Centre for Health Promotion.

Richardson, S. A. (1976). Attitudes and behavior toward the physically handicapped. In D. Bergsma & A. E. Pulver (Eds.), *Developmental disabilities: Psychologic and social implications* (pp. 15-34). New York: Alan R. Liss.

Richardson, S. A. (1983). Children's values in regard to disabilities: A reply to Yuker. *Rehabilitation Psychology, 28,* 131-140.

Robinson, M., & Thompson, T. N. (1980). PHAB and the integration process. *Journal of Leisurability, 7*(3), 26-35.

Rodin, G., Craven, J., & Littlefield, C. (1991). *Depression in the medically ill: An integrated approach.* New York: Brunner/Mazel.

Rodin, M. (1982). Non-engagement, failure to engage, and disengagement. In S. W. Duck (Ed.), *Personal relationships 4: Dissolving personal relationships* (pp. 31-50). London: Academic Press.

Rogers, P., & Kreutzer, J. (1984). Family crises following head injury: A network strategy. *Journal of Neuroscience Nursing, 16*, 340-446.

Roloff, M. E. (1981). *Interpersonal communication: The social exchange approach*. Beverly Hills, CA: Sage.

Romano, J. M., & Turner, J. A. (1985). Chronic pain and depression: Does the evidence support a relationship? *Psychological Bulletin, 97*, 18-34.

Romano, J. M., Turner, J. A., Friedman, L. S., Bulcroft, R. A., Jenson, M. A., & Hopps, H. (1991). Observational assessment of chronic pain patient spouse behavioral interactions. *Behavioral Therapy, 1*, 271-283.

Rook, K. S. (1987). Social support versus companionship: Effects of life stress, loneliness, and evaluations by others. *Journal of Personality and Social Psychology, 47*, 1132-1147.

Rook, K. S. (1990). Social relationships as a source of companionship: Implications for older adults' psychological wellbeing. In I. G. Sarason, B. R. Sarason, & G. R. Pierce (Eds.), *Social support: An interactional view: Issues in social support research* (pp. 219-250). New York: John Wiley.

Rook, K. S. (1992). Detrimental aspects of social relationships. In H. O. Veiel & U. Baumann (Eds.), *Meaning and measurement of social support* (pp. 157-159). New York: Hemisphere.

Rose, S., & Serafica, F. C. (1986). Keeping and ending casual, close and best friendships. *Journal of Social and Personal Relationships, 3*, 275-288.

Rosenstiel, A. K., & Keefe, F. J. (1983). The use of coping strategies in chronic low back pain patients: Relationship to patient characteristics and current adjustment. *Pain, 17*, 33-44.

Rubenstein, C. M., & Shaver, P. (1982). The experience of loneliness. In L. A. Peplau & D. Perlman (Eds.), *Loneliness: A sourcebook of current theory, research and therapy* (pp. 206-224). New York: John Wiley.

Ruddick, S. (1989). *Maternal thinking: Toward a politics of peace*. Boston: Beacon.

Rusbult, C. E., & Buunk, B. P. (1993). Commitment processes in close relationships: An interdependence analysis. *Journal of Social and Personal Relationships, 10*, 175-204.

Russell, S. (1985). *Social implications of multiple sclerosis*. Final report of a formulation grant from the National Health Research and Development Program, Health and Welfare Canada.

Sapadin, L. A. (1988). Friendship and gender: Perspectives of professional men and women. *Journal of Social and Personal Relationships, 5*, 387-403.

Sarason, I. G., Pierce, G. R., & Sarason, B. R. (1990). Social support and interpersonal processes: A triadic hypothesis. *Journal of Social and Personal Relationships, 7*, 495-506.

Sargent, J. (1985). Juvenile diabetes mellitus and the family. In P. I. Ahmed & N. Ahmed (Eds.), *Coping with juvenile diabetes* (pp. 205-233). Springfield, IL: Charles C Thomas.

Satariano, W. A., & Syme, S. L. (1981). Life changes and disease in elderly populations: Coping with change. In G. H. March (Ed.), *Aging: Biology and behavior* (pp. 311-328). New York: Academic Press.

Schmaling, K. B., & Jacobson, N. S. (1988). Recent developments in family behavioral marital therapy. *Contemporary Family Therapy, 10,* 17-29.

Shaw, S. M. (1985). The meaning of leisure in everyday life. *Leisure Sciences, 7,* 1-24.

Shears, L. M., & Jensema, C. J. (1969). Social acceptability of anomolous persons. *Exceptional Children, 35,* 91-96.

Shontz, F. C. (1978). Theories about the adjustment to having a disability. In W. Cruickshank (Ed.), *Psychology of exceptional children and youth* (pp. 3-44). Englewood Cliffs, NJ: Prentice Hall.

Shulman, N. (1975). Life cycle variations in patterns of close relationships. *Journal of Marriage and the Family, 37,* 813-821.

Silver, R. C., Wortman, C. B., & Crofton, C. (1990). The role of coping in support provision: The self-representation dilemma of victims of life crises. In B. R. Sarason, I. G. Sarason, & G. R. Pierce (Eds.), *Social support: An interactional view* (pp. 397-426). New York: John Wiley.

Simmons, S., & Ball, S. E. (1984). Marital adjustment and self actualization in couples married before and after spinal cord injury. *Journal of Marriage and the Family, 44,* 943-945.

Simpson, E. L. (1982). *Notes on an emergency: A journal of recovery.* New York: Norton.

Smith, M. D., Hong, B. A., & Robson, A. M. (1985). Diagnosis of major depression in patients with end stage renal disease: Comparative analysis. *American Journal of Medicine, 79,* 160-166.

Smith, R. T. (1980). Use of social resources by the disabled: Primary and secondary group influences. *International Journal of Rehabilitation Research, 3,* 469-483.

Social Trends Directorate. (1986). *Profile of disabled persons in Canada.* Ottawa: Statistics Canada.

Sourkes, B. M. (1982). *The deepening shade: Psychological aspects of life threatening illness.* Pittsburgh: University of Pittsburgh Press.

Speedling, E. J. (1982). *Heart attack: The family response at home and in the hospital.* New York: Tavistock.

Spitzberg, B. H., & Brunner, C. C. (1991). Toward a theoretical integration of context and competence inference research. *Western Journal of Speech Communication, 55,* 28-46.

Statistics Canada. (1992, October). 1991 Health and Activity Limitation Survey—Amended Oct. 13, 1992. *The Daily.* Ottawa: Statistics Canada.

Steuve, C. A., & Gerson, K. (1977). Personal relations across the life cycle. In C. S. Fischer (Ed.), *Networks and places: Social relations in the urban setting* (pp. 79-98). New York: Free Press.

Stewart, M. J. (1993). *Integrating social support in nursing.* Newbury Park, CA: Sage.

Strauss, A. L., Corbin, J., Fagerhaugh, S., Gleason, B., Maines, D., Suczek, B., & Wiener, C. (1984). *Chronic illness and the quality of life.* St. Louis, MO: C. V. Mosby.

Sullivan, M. J. L., Edgley, K., Mikail, S., Dehoux, E., & Fisher, R. (1992). Psychological correlates of health care utilization in chronic illness. *Canadian Journal of Rehabilitation, 6,* 13-21.

Sullivan, M. J. L., Mikail, S., & Weinshenker, B. (1992, November). *Marital dysfunction, depression, and multiple sclerosis.* Paper presented at the annual meeting of the Atlantic Rehabilitation Association, Halifax, Nova Scotia.

Sullivan, M. J. L., Reesor, K., Mikail, S., & Fisher, R. (1992). The treatment of depression in chronic low back pain: Review and recommendations. *Pain, 50,* 5-13.

Taylor, C. B., Bandura, A., Ewart, C. K., Miller, N. H., & DeBusk, R. F. (1985). Exercise testing to enhance wives' confidence in their husband's cardiac capacity soon after clinically uncomplicated acute myocardial infarction. *American Journal of Cardiology, 55,* 635-38.

Taylor, S. E., & Crocker, J. (1981). Schematic bases of social information processing. In E. T. Higgins, C. P. Herman, & M. P. Zanna (Eds.), *Social cognition: The Ontario Symposium, Vol. 1* (pp. 89-134). Hillsdale, NJ: Lawrence Erlbaum.

Thibaut, J. W., & Kelley, H. H. (1959). *The social psychology of small groups.* New York: John Wiley.

Thoits, P. A. (1982). Conceptual, methodological, and theoretical problems in studying social support as a buffer against life stress. *Journal of Health and Social Behavior, 23,* 145-159.

Thoits, P. A. (1991). Gender differences in coping with emotional distress. In J. Eckenrode (Ed.), *The social context of coping* (pp. 107-131). New York: Plenum.

Thompson, E. H., & Doll, W. (1982). The burden of families coping with the mentally ill: An invisible crisis. *Family Relations, 31,* 379-388.

Toseland, R., Rossiter, C., & Labrecque, M. (1989). The effectiveness of three group intervention strategies to support family caregivers. *American Journal of Orthopsychiatry, 59,* 420-429.

Treischmann, R. (1974). Coping and disability: A sliding scale of goals. *Archives of Physical Medicine & Rehabilitation, 55,* 556-560.

Turk, D. C., & Kerns, R. D. (1985). *Health, illness, and families.* New York: John Wiley.

Turk, D. C., Rudy, T. E., & Flor, H. (1985). Why a family perspective for pain? *International Journal of Family Therapy, 7,* 223-234.

Turner, H. A., Hays, R. B., & Coates, T. J. (1993). Determinants of social support among gay men: The context of AIDS. *Journal of Health and Social Behaviour, 34,* 37-53.

Turner, J. A., & Clancy, S. (1986). Strategies for coping with low back pain: Relationship to pain and disability. *Pain, 24,* 355-364.

U.S. Bureau of the Census. (1986). *Disability, functional limitation and health insurance coverage: 1984-85.* Washington, DC: Government Printing Office.

Utne, M. K., Hatfield, E., Traupmann, J., & Greenberger, D. (1984). Equity, marital satisfaction, and stability. *Journal of Social and Personal Relationships, 1,* 323-332.

Van Uitert, D., Eberly, R., & Engdahl, R. (1985, August). *Stress and coping of wives following their husbands' strokes.* Paper presented at the annual meeting of the American Psychological Association, Los Angeles.

Vaughn, C. E., & Leff, J. P. (1976). The influence of family and social factors on the course of psychiatric illness. *British Journal of Psychiatry, 129,* 125-137.

Vaughn, C. E., Snyder, K. S., Freeman, W., Jones, S., & Faloon, I. R. H. (1984). Family factors in schizophrenia relapse. *Archives of General Psychiatry, 41,* 1169-1171.

Viney, L. (1989). A constructivist model of psychological reactions to physical illness and injury. In G. J. Neimeyer & R. A. Neimeyer (Eds.), *Advances in personal construct psychology* (Vol. 1, pp. 117-151). Greenwich, CT: JAI.

Vitaliano, P. P., Katon, W., Russo, J., Maiuro, R. D., Anderson, K., & Jones, M. (1987). Coping as an index of illness behavior in panic disorder. *Journal of Nervous and Mental Disease, 175,* 78-84.

Vitaliano, P. P., Maiuro, R. D., Russo, J., Katon, W., DeWolfe, D., & Hall, G. (1990). Coping profiles associated with psychiatric, physical, health, work, and family problems. *Health Psychology, 9,* 348-376.

Vonnegut, K. (1989, June). Kurt Vonnegut. *Lear's,* p. 71.

Walker, K. N., MacBride, A., & Vachon, M. L. (1977). Social support networks in the crisis of bereavement. *Social Science and Medicine, 11,* 35-42.

Walters, M., Carter, B., Papp, P., & Silverstein, O. (1988). *The invisible web.* New York: Guilford.

Watzlawick, P., Weakland, J., & Fisch, R. (1974). *Change: Principles of problem formation and problem resolution.* New York: Norton.

Watzlawick, P. W., & Coyne, J. C. (1980). Depression following stroke: Brief problem-focused family treatment. *Family Process, 19,* 13-18.

Weakland, J. (1977). Family somatics: A neglected edge. *Family Process, 16,* 263-272.

Weinberg, N., & Williams, J. (1978). How the physically disabled perceive their disabilities. *Journal of Rehabilitation, 44,* 31-33.

Weissman, M. M. (1975). The assessment of social adjustment: A review of techniques. *Archives of General Psychiatry, 32,* 357-365.

Weissman, M. M., Sholomskas, D., & John, K. (1981). The assessment of social adjustment: An update. *Archives of General Psychiatry, 38,* 1250-1258.

Weiss, R. S. (1974). The provisions of social relationships. In Z. Rubin (Ed.), *Doing unto others* (pp. 17-26). Englewood Cliffs, NJ: Prentice Hall.

Wellisch, D., Mosher, M., & Scoy, C. (1978). Management of family emotional stress: Family group therapy in a private oncology practice. *International Journal of Group Psychotherapy, 28,* 225-231.

Wellman, B. (1985). Domestic work, paid work, and net work. In S. W. Duck & D. Perlman (Eds.), *Understanding personal relationships* (pp. 159-191). London: Sage.

Wellman, B., & Wellman, B. (1992). Domestic affairs and network relations. *Journal of Social and Personal Relationships, 9,* 385-409.

Wheaton, B. (1990). Where work and family meet: Stress across social roles. In J. Eckenrode & S. Gore (Eds.), *Stress between work and family* (pp. 153-174). New York: Plenum.

White, C. (1994). *Companionate activity adjustment in multiple sclerosis.* Unpublished master's thesis, Dalhousie University, Halifax, Nova Scotia.

White, M., & Epston, D. (1990). *Narrative means to therapeutic ends.* New York: Norton.

Wiseman, J. (1986). Friendship bonds and binds in a voluntary relationship. *Journal of Social and Personal Relationships, 3,* 191-211.

Wolcott, D. L., Namir, S., Fawzy, F. I., Gottlieb, M. S., & Mitsuyasu, R. T. (1986). Illness concerns, attitudes towards homosexuality, and social support in gay men with AIDS. *General Hospital Psychiatry, 8,* 395-403.

Wolfensberger, W. (1972). *The principles of normalization in human services.* Toronto: National Institute on Mental Retardation.

Wood, J. T. (1993). Engendered relations: Interaction, caring, power, and responsibility in intimacy. In S. Duck (Ed.), *Social context and relationships* (pp. 26-54). Newbury Park, CA: Sage.

Worchel, S. (1984). The darker side of helping: The social dynamics of helping and cooperation. In E. Staub, D. Bar-Tal, J. Karylowski, & J. Reykowski (Eds.), *Development and maintenance of prosocial behavior* (pp. 379-396). New York: Plenum.

World Health Organization. (1980). *International classification of impairments, disabilities and impairments: A manual of classification relating to the consequences of disease.* Geneva: Author.

Wortman, C. B., & Conway, T. L. (1985). The role of social support in adaptation and recovery from physical illness. In S. Cohen & S. L. Syme (Eds.), *Social support and health* (pp. 61-82). New York: Academic Press.

Wright, B. A. (1975). Social psychology leads to enhanced rehabilitation effectiveness. *Rehabilitation Counseling Bulletin, 18,* 214-223.

Wright, B. A. (1980). Developing constructive views of life with a disability. *Rehabilitation Literature, 41*(11-12), 274-279.

Wright, B. A. (1983). *Physical disability—A psycho-social approach* (2nd ed.). New York: Harper & Row.

Young, R. F. (1983). The family-illness intermesh: Theoretical aspects and their application. *Social Science and Medicine, 17,* 395-398.

Yuker, H. (1983). The lack of a stable order of preference for disabilities: A response to Richardson and Ronald. *Rehabilitation Psychology, 28,* 93-104.

Yuker, H. E., Block, J. R., & Young, J. H. (1966). *The measurement of attitudes toward disabled persons* (Human Resources Study No. 7). Albertson, NY: Human Resources.

Zarit, S. H., Todd, P. A., & Zarit, J. M. (1986). Subjective burden of husbands and wives as caregivers: A longitudinal study. *The Gerontologist, 26,* 260-266.

Zigler, E., & Hall, N. (1986). Mainstreaming and the philosophy of normalization. In C. J. Meisel (Ed.), *Mainstreaming handicapped children: Outcomes, controversies and new directions* (pp. 21-42). Hillsdale, NJ: Lawrence Erlbaum.

Zola, I. (1981). Communication barriers between "the able-bodied" and "the handicapped." *Archives of Physical Medicine and Rehabilitation, 62,* 355-359.

Author Index

Ablin, A. R., 41, 78
Abrams, D. B., 105
Adams, A. E., 59
Adams, J. E., 83
Adams, R. G., 9, 43
Adler, D. L., 11
Ahern, D. K., 59
Aldwin, C., 82
Allan, G. A., 123, 136
Allen, B., 93
Allen, K. R., 67
Alpert, R., 50
Altschuler, J., 113
American Psychiatric Association, 31
Amsel, R., 27, 28
Anderson, B., 99
Anderson, B. A., 74, 100
Anderson, C. M., 106

Anderson, D., 54
Anderson, K., 83
Anderson, M. P., 106
Antonucci, T. C., 39
Argyle, M., 50, 61
Ashkanazi, G. H., 50
Atcherson, E., 31
Athelstan, G. T., 59
Atkins, C. J., 83
Atwood, C., 31

Babchuk, N., 70
Baird, M., 100, 111
Baker, L., 100, 110
Ball, S. E., 58, 59
Bandura, A., 99
Banfield, E. C., 92

Subject Index

About the Authors

Renee F. Lyons is Associate Professor in the School of Recreation, Physical and Health Education, Dalhousie University, Halifax, Nova Scotia, Canada. She received her master's degree in Counseling Psychology from Xavier University, Cincinnati, Ohio, and her doctorate in Leisure Studies (lifestyle adjustment and disability) from the University of Oregon. Her research interests concern coping and adaptational processes in chronic illness and disability, particularly issues of personal relationships, and she has written extensively in this area. She is particularly interested in the use of personal accounts in examining the experience of serious health problems and adaptational strategies, as well as shared or communal coping strategies for dealing with stressful life events.

Michael J. L. Sullivan is Associate Professor of Psychology at Dalhousie University. He received his doctorate from Concordia University in 1988. His research focuses on emotional factors in disability and the relationship between depression and social cognition. He has published more than 30 papers on topics related to health psychology, social cognition, and disability. He is also a practicing clinician working primarily with couples in distress. He claims that one day he will abandon academia and clinical psychology to become a very rich and famous folk singer.

Paul G. Ritvo, Ph.D., C. Psych., is Assistant Professor, Department of Behavioural Science, Faculty of Medicine, University of Toronto. He is Principal Investigator of the Sociobehavioral Cancer Research Centre at The Toronto Hospital, the Princess Margaret Hospital, and the University of Toronto and funded by the National Cancer Institute of Canada, and a staff health psychologist at The Toronto Hospital.

James C. Coyne is a Professor of Psychology in the Departments of Family Practice and Psychiatry at the University of Michigan Medical School. He received his doctorate from Indiana University in 1975. In addition to numerous articles and chapters, he coauthored *Father Knows Best: Use and Abuse of Power in Freud's Case of Dora* and edited *Essential Papers on Depression.* He is best known for his work on interpersonal aspects of depression, but other current research interests include individual and family aspects of genetic testing for risk of early onset of breast cancer and couples coping with congestive heart failure. After receiving considerable feedback from audiences throughout North America and Europe, he no longer anticipates being able to quit academia to become a rich and famous Irish folk singer.